Early praise for T

**The perfect guide to joini
meaning of wealth**

Mr. Matthews has written an extremely valuable book bringing together two subjects rarely connected: money and Buddhism. His background both as an economist / business owner combined with many years as a student and teacher of meditation creates the perfect seat from which to present this material.

Bringing together the view of both inherent wealth and material wealth as it relates to the traditional teaching of the Four Noble Truths first presented by the Buddha creates the perfect framework for looking closely at the meaning of human worthiness, what we value, where richness comes from, and ultimately how this relates to our money and livelihood.

Based on teachings he presented to audiences over the course of his teachings series, Mr. Matthews' book provides a helpful and insightful treatment of these topics that will benefit both new students and long time practitioners of meditation and Buddhism. I'm so pleased to see this book now available to a wide audience so that the teachings of inherent human goodness can be brought to the world of wealth and money.

—ROBERT REICHNER, CEO, *RepairShopr and Kalapa Envoy for Enrichment*

Wise and uplifting
Layth Matthews has written a very wise and uplifting book about what it truly means to be a wealthy person. Inspired by Buddhist teachings, Layth shows us how to remove the obstacles that prevent us from seeing our own inherent prosperity. With humor and compassion this highly readable book encourages us to take a more direct path to the real goal: a wealthy state of mind.

—DR. JUSTINE NOEL, *Professor of Philosophy and Religious Studies, Camosun College*

Engaging and highly useful
A brief, engaging and highly useful approach to dealing with money in a wise, spiritually informed way. I recommend this book to anyone who wants to actually live the real challenges and opportunities of life as path.

—JAMES SACAMANO, MD, *Author of Getting Back to Wholeness, The Treasure of Inner Health and the Power of a Meaningful Life*

Generous and helpful
Layth Matthews offers us all the gift of a new way of looking at our relationship to money, wealth and abundance. The book presents practical pointers on how to contemplate our attitudes to materialism, livelihood, and the inherent richness in our lives. Fantastic!

—DEBRA ROSS, *Manager, Outreach and Partnerships, College of Sustainability, Dalhousie University*

Delightful, insightful and practical
A delightful, insightful and practical book about inner and outer wealth; it's a cheerful read about a very important topic. While it's accessible for the average reader interested in examining their economic values, it's also a doorway into understanding Buddhist philosophy and practice. A refreshing antidote to our materialist world, Layth's book delivers practical wisdom with a sense of humour.

—MANDY LEITH, *Digital Producer, Founder and Director of OPEN CINEMA*

Eminently readable and applicable
... succinct and insightful prose delivered with a relaxed and charming wit.... Practical examples and an obvious depth. The first paragraph on page 50 alone was worth the cover price. I recommend this book to everyone and anyone.

—MIKE LENZ, *Business Coach*

Inspiring and brilliant!
It is the type of book that you should savour each chapter like a good piece of pie ... but I read it in a day because I couldn't put it down. Each chapter has everyday comparisons that resonated with my own perspective ... very easy to read and understand. Based on a series of lectures, I feel as though I were in attendance after reading it. Individuals from all walks of life, experience and denomination would benefit from reading and that's a wonderful gift!

—COLLEEN MACNEIL

The Four
Noble Truths
of
Wealth

a Buddhist view of economic life

Layth Matthews

Library and Archives Canada Cataloguing in Publication
Matthews, Layth, 1962–
    The Four Noble Truths of wealth : a Buddhist view of economic life / Layth Matthews.

ISBN 978-0-9918023-0-2

    1. Wealth--Religious aspects--Buddhism. 2. Four Noble Truths.
3. Meditation--Buddhism. I. Title.
BQ4570.W4M38 2013   294.3'4435   C2013-900454-8

Editing by Julia Fabian
Cover design by Silas Rosenblatt
Book design by Fiona Raven

First Printing, January 2014
Printed in United States of America

Published by Enlightened Economy Books
info@enlightenedeconomy.com

www.EnlightenedEconomy.com

To Sakyong Mipham Rinpoche,
holder of the Shambhala Buddhist Lineage

and

To my Father,
who has given me the best of both worlds

Contents

Introduction

The great investor Warren Buffet once said, 'if you don't know how to manage $100 you won't know how to manage $100,000'. With a little transcendental accounting, we can restate this from the Buddhist perspective to say, "if you know how to appreciate a moment, you will know how to appreciate a lifetime".

The Buddhist advice for economic life is the same as for every other aspect of life: start with the view. The idea is that understanding the foundations of a situation, in this case the human condition, helps us to make better choices going forward.

All human beings wish to be happy and free from suffering. The Buddhist approach is to contemplate the nature of happiness and suffering themselves as the means to navigate toward a more joyful existence and the elimination of suffering. Here suffering is distinguished from pain as the misery that comes from being habitually unable to appreciate things as they are.

Economic life is often regarded as a necessary evil to support true spirituality or material comfort, but that is a shame because seeing the economic aspect of life as a spiritual path has great potential to help us cheer up.

Economic setbacks can even be opportune for contemplating the nature of economic life and wealth itself. It's much easier to overlook the subtleties of our experience when times are good, and taming the mind in the face of uncertainty has profound benefits for oneself and others.

Seeing the economic aspect of life as a spiritual path has great potential to help us cheer up.

This book is based on a series of five public talks given at the Hope Lutheran Church in Nanaimo, B.C. beginning in the autumn of 2008; and one open house talk at the Victoria Shambhala Centre in July 2012. The introductory talk in the Nanaimo series went unrecorded, so the Victoria talk is included to take its place.

All of these were offered as public talks without prerequisites; as such, each one starts with an introduction or review. I hope that you will find this iterative approach clarifying and reinforcing as we comb through the key ideas with different examples again and again.

Buddhist teachings are sometimes divided into the stages of view, practice, and action. View is the most fundamental of these because the other stages depend on it. This book provides an introduction to meditation as the highest best vehicle to establish a wealthy outlook, which is the first step and the fruition of genuine prosperity.

Inherent Wealth

Based on an open house talk at the Victoria Shambhala Centre, July 18th, 2012.

With these open house talks we try to bridge the gap between the meditation cushion and day-to-day life experience. That's kind of what the path of meditation is all about. Essentially we practice bringing our minds back to where our bodies are so we can do it more easily the rest of the time.

Sometimes we say the path of meditation is not the practice of being back, it's the practice of coming back. So when you catch your mind wandering in your sitting practice, you've already succeeded. You don't have to beat yourself up because you were on daydream vacation for 10 minutes—you're back.

We could bring our attention back to where we are at any point in our day. The essence of meditation, the way we practice it, is simply training ourselves to be biased toward being present. We want to remove any obstacles to just being here, which is very powerful. That is what we discover when we meditate.

We are constantly crisscrossing the road of being present in our daily lives already. There are moments when we've got to cross the street or chop an onion which require us to be completely in our bodies, completely here. These are just mundane moments of awareness, yet they are like gateways to something extremely wholesome and significant.

We could bring our attention back to where we are at any point in our day.

It's easy to take these little check-ins for granted without recognizing those moments or becoming familiar with what it's like to be completely here, much less even value it. But meditators like us have discovered over thousands of years that just being present is actually a very profound thing. Most of us come to give meditation a try because we have a hunch that maybe being present is a good thing to do—enough of a hunch that we're willing to experiment, we're willing to try it.

So when we're on the cushion, we're really just practicing being back. We say to ourselves, "Instead of following every train of thought, I'm going to just keep my mind and body together and see what happens. I'm going to lean into being present a little bit, keep that window open a little longer, a little more often."

By applying ourselves to the technique of sitting meditation, which is just noticing thoughts and returning to the present over and over, we become familiar with what it's like to be where we are, and who we are as well. That creates a whole different relationship with the world. It's living life with a lot of fresh starts. Each time you return to just being where you are, it's a fresh start. You can look at your experience with new eyes.

What's unusual about meditation is that we are not following the content of our thoughts like we normally do. Normally, we just swing from one storyline, one stream of thought, to another, right? And then we drop one and work on another one. Like a puppy hiding chew toys around the house. We chew on the office politics bone for a while and then we'll chew on the family dynamics shoe or whatever preoccupies us, going from one to the other, avoiding any gaps as we attempt to work our way through stuff.

> *Each time you return to just being*
> *where you are, it's a fresh start.*

We have our favorite ways to keep ourselves preoccupied and we habitually keep busy with something—it almost doesn't matter what. There's the presumption that if we ever stop thinking about stuff it would just be dead air.

What meditation allows us to do is look at how mind operates to look at the overall activity of our mind, rather than just the content du jour, the argument du jour, the hope du jour, the fear du jour.

Meditation gives us the chance to see how mind works and its patterns, because we are creating a vast space. We are making things very simple, creating a clean white backdrop of stillness against which to see and feel what's going on more objectively.

> *What meditation allows us to do*
> *is look at how mind operates.*

Tonight we're going to apply that same spacious approach to wealth. Tonight's talk is called "Inherent Wealth."

External Wealth

The first step toward understanding wealth is to explore our relationship with prosperity. We need to contemplate the definition of prosperity and how we approach it opposed to just conjuring up the next strategy to pay the bills or make a million.

The pursuit of wealth is a ubiquitous pre-occupation even though we don't always think of it as a pursuit. Mostly we just think we are trying to keep ourselves out of trouble or one step ahead. But these are just different episodes of a formulaic mental subtext that reiterates constantly.

One reason we get stuck on this track is that nobody is really qualified to talk about wealth. Somebody who's poor or been bankrupt is not really qualified to talk about wealth because they haven't gotten themselves out of the ditch, obviously, so what do they know? Somebody who's rich is not exactly qualified to talk about wealth, because they might be far removed from the practical realities that normal people face. And then somebody who's middle class, they don't know much about either end of the spectrum, right? In all of these cases we are triangulating toward the same floating island of relative wealth.

That's an example of how habitual mind works. We're in this windswept place where we doubt our own experience but can't quite trust anyone else's either. So we default to shortsighted strategies without giving much thought to the bigger picture. As a result, we are constantly seeking external solutions to internal problems. There are external aspects of our lives that can help us connect with a sense of prosperity, but not for long if we view them the wrong way.

We are constantly seeking external solutions to internal problems.

Meditation creates a great big space so that we can eventually see the recurring patterns of our thoughts and mental projections. Without that vast perspective, we have been looking at the movie of our thoughts without realizing that mind is the movie-making machine. So it always seems like a new movie could keep us in balance, when in fact our own minds are directing our interpretation of everything.

We have been looking at the movie of our thoughts without realizing that mind is the movie-making machine.

Wealth is elusive like that too. Wealth by external definitions is: hard to come by, hard to keep, and subject to depreciation and inflation. It's a slippery thing. The internal value of external wealth, whether you monetize it or think of it as a car, house, status, or a relationship, can also change instantly. Like the minute you drive a new car off the sales lot. Not only does it depreciate in external value, but you have a different relationship to it internally as well. With an acquisitive mentality, anything that you acquire doesn't mean quite as much to you, once you have acquired it.

The key point is that external wealth is not more legitimate than what we might call internal wealth, because it's constantly changing. There's a struggle involved and there is even an assumption that if there's no struggle, it must not be valuable, or it's more valuable if it is a struggle. That is a self-perpetuating frame of mind, which you will explore when you take the "Contentment in Everyday Life" class. Contentment is not something you can realize by chasing it you know.

The external approach to wealth overlooks how mind operates and the role of perception. It is like being an insecure mountain climber with his back to the view, thinking about what you haven't accomplished all the time. Maybe you put up a picture of your favorite object on your desk and dream about acquiring it as a motivational technique. But that mentality is counterproductive from an internal wealth point of view because it distracts you from the richness of where you are and takes you out of balance. Even if you eventually achieve your goal, you might build up the habit of overlooking a lot.

Contentment is not something you can realize by chasing it you know.

We have to watch out for our mentality around goals. Which is not to say we shouldn't have goals or appreciate fine things, but we have to understand the mind aspect. We have to look at how our minds play into whatever it is that we are aspiring to, whether it's excellent fitness or amazing amounts of money.

So there's this tug of war that goes on between the internal and the external value of where we are physically, psychologically, and socially. We think that there shouldn't be any longing or that there doesn't have to be a struggle with economic life, but there aren't a lot of people who can say, "I'm completely satisfied with where I am." and really mean it.

Even if one is satisfied, there is still maintenance. You might feel you have to maintain the satisfaction. How are you going to stay there? How are you going to protect it? How are you going to protect your family? Sometimes being very wealthy, leads one to live in a very defensive way. Like a flower garden surrounded by a high fence, the world has actually gotten smaller with increased wealth. You can see that when travelling. The nicer the hotel you stay in, the fewer people you meet. If you go to the youth hostel, you meet everybody! So even if you deem yourself to be a success, there is constant mental coaching that goes on with respect to maintenance. Rather than liberating yourself, you have simply succeeded in reshuffling anxieties.

*The nicer the hotel you stay in,
the fewer people you meet.*

Despite the conflicting evidence, we still assume that success would be a non-stop holiday if we just get it right. We think, "If I only won the lottery, my life would be great!" We don't actually think about it in detail. If you stop and reflect on the historical experience of big lottery winners and pop stars, you might not be so sure.

Like atmospheric pressure, wherever we are in life also shapes us into who we are. Sudden changes are like spinning a roulette wheel with everything, including what we love. So the key is learning to fully appreciate where we are vs. pining for something new, which is coming anyway, and very soon.

*Like atmospheric pressure, wherever we are
in life also shapes us into who we are.*

Nevertheless, it's common to assume that a big material change would be a shortcut to happiness. Ironically, this assumption leads us to miss immediate opportunities, squandering money by speculating in the stock market or spending $10 on lottery tickets with a sub-atomic chance of success. I did that last week, so I can speak from experience. Thank goodness, we didn't win!

External wealth is completely relative and it is a dream. The reality is much different. The proof of this is that the comforts and financial security most of us enjoy right now would be like a lottery win—amazing prosperity—for most of the world's population, not just orphaned children in Africa.

Our situation e.g. clean drinking water out of the garden hose, is already so cushy, it's simply amazing, even in a relative sense. Despite this our minds are habituated to see things comparatively, so we keep raising the bar until whatever we have is insufficient. This attitude also makes us reluctant to welcome others "yet". We are waiting for when we can "afford to". It seems normal to think in terms of self-protection and advantage, because everyone else is doing it. With this mentality, the wow factor of any increase in funds is more than consumed by the increase in expectations that accompany it.

It seems normal to think in terms of self-protection and advantage, because everyone else is doing it.

It's easy to overlook the isolation aspect when fantasizing about being financially "secure". In reality, newfound wealth challenges relationships and complicates friendships we might otherwise enjoy more freely. New resources bring new obligations and suspicions. It's a frequent challenge for people, trying to manage new money for themselves.

So it's easy to overvalue external success—net worth, credentials, jobs, partners—by assuming a "worry-free" state of mind will come along with it. Remaining ignorant of our minds, economic life is just lining up for the Ferris wheel again and again. Even if we achieve the object of our desire, and even if it is supportive, the mindset of acquisition undercuts the whole thing. The consequences of habitually thinking in a certain way far exceed the benefits of any situation we might get ourselves into, because every situation is temporary.

Unconditional Wealth

From the Buddhist point of view, human beings are inherently healthy, wealthy, and wise. The essence of wealthiness is peace of mind and confidence. We imagine wealthiness in this way, but then think, "if only I had enough money, fame, and power to get there."

From the Buddhist point of view, human beings are inherently healthy, wealthy, and wise.

Of course, we could manage the worry faucet for ourselves, work with our state of mind directly, right now. But somehow doing it for oneself does not seem legitimate. The habitual expectation that something else is needed is the greatest challenge to wealthiness.

If your confidence is based on situations or objects, then you're immediately living in fear, because what if whatever you're counting on falls apart? What if your property is not there? What if somebody else wants it, or tries to take it? Maybe they will; most of us have the same delusions as you.

Philanthropic aspiration is another rationalization for fixating on external wealth. If you spend or donate your money wisely, that can be very helpful. But that's not as easy as it looks. Solving problems with money can also distract your beneficiaries from developing the essential outlook, disciplines, and resourcefulness that will help them most in the long run.

In my work as a mortgage broker, we do a lot of refinancing to consolidate debts. It's a great fresh start, but if you don't recognize the ongoing discipline needed to manage money wisely, you won't get anywhere, no matter how many revolutions you create.

On the other hand, if you have discipline, faith, and determination, it is possible to work with the most overwhelming problems. The place to begin is by taking full responsibility for your own sense of well-being. The foundation of genuine discipline is making friends with oneself.

*The foundation of genuine discipline
is making friends with oneself.*

Not recognizing our inherent completeness, we are habituated to seek success through external objects. Peace of mind, confidence, and the ability to help others are expected to come along like fringe benefits of wealth and power. Ironically, these things are not fringe benefits, but rather the essence of genuine wealth and power in themselves. We can expand these capacities most directly by working with mind.

Synchronizing body and mind connects us to our innate wisdom, which brings great benefit. This kind of wisdom is characterized by humor, intelligence, and a sense of capacity that is very nearly, if not exactly, the essence of wealth. We access it by just being present. Really being present creates a vast space in which penetrating wisdom can occur.

It's kind of scary, actually, to just be present, which is why we don't hang out there much. It's very unbounded like Tarzan letting go of one vine without grasping onto another right away. "Space" here essentially means without ego, so it can feel desolate at times, but it's also very electric. Without training we respond to any kind of un-confirming space with panic. We can't get past the "dead air", "uncomfortable silence", or "boredom". But learning to hangout with uncertainty is the direct path to peace of mind and confidence.

Learning to hangout with uncertainty is the direct path to peace of mind and confidence.

That's what the Great Eastern Sun on the Shambhala banner represents. It represents the bringing together of body and mind and the confidence that comes from doing that.

The Buddhist point of view is that genuine wealth is inherent to human beings. The question is not how to get it, but how to remove obstacles to connecting with it. That is a more accurate way of approaching the whole wealth challenge, internally and externally, because it's a better understanding of what we want to get from our lives. How can we remove obstacles to perceiving the prosperity inherent within us, and all around us?

The view and implication of inherent wealth is that we are already as wealthy as we are ever going to be on the level that matters. We're already as rich as Bill Gates (*audience member: "nice"*) in the sense that Bill Gates is human too.

We are already as wealthy as we are ever going to be on the level that matters.

Since even external wealth must come in through our perceptions and interpretations, it may be more straightforward to contemplate wealth as a state of mind. It doesn't matter what it is, your dream house or car, your original Picasso—all wealth is a form of perception.

From this vantage point, the subtler the degree of your perception, the richer you are. The more you slow down your neurotic mental speed, the wealthier you become, because your perception increases. Opening up reveals the diamond-like qualities of ordinary experience: the richness of the floorboards, the sounds of the birds, or the ironically ripe smell of the compost facility on Pleasant Street. That's it.

In terms of the human experience, there are two ways to get rich. One is to get more treasure. The other is to expand your definition of treasure, which is a really good idea since that is going to be the determining factor no matter how much money you've got. More perception equals more wealth, subject only to the capacity to appreciate it. Wealth is what you can appreciate. So there's a high return on investment for working on the appreciation bit.

Wealth is what you can appreciate.

Creating Enlightened Economy

In Shambhala we like to contemplate creating enlightened society. So the last thing I want to say about wealth is that the way we define and pursue wealth personally has a great deal of influence on our world. You can see how poverty, warfare, and environmental degradation tie in to confusion about wealth. It boils down to ignorance about mind.

Because we don't realize that we actually can and must work with our own state of mind, we do all kinds of frivolous things that perpetuate this reckless consumer society. Everything you see has got some logic or intelligence supporting it somewhere, of course. But much of our world is neurotically prioritized.

What gets publicized, what succeeds, even which restaurants make it in town, is a reflection of how we feel about ourselves. Once we have made a connection to inherent wealth, we are not so desperate for the most immediate form of comfort. We are not thinking so small or short-term. We have more of a "seat" in our lives, a monarch's perspective, which makes us not so speedy, because we see more of the landscape. This broader view doesn't exclude anything in particular, but illuminates more choices. Saner choices organically reshape the economy.

In an enlightened society, there would probably still be fast food, but it would probably be a lot "slower food" because people would have more respect for themselves. A lot of what succeeds in our world is a reflection of us not having made friends with ourselves on a deep level.

A lot of what succeeds in our world is a reflection of us not having made friends with ourselves on a deep level.

Q. *Can you talk about how generosity fits into that? I understand that Chögyam Trungpa said that we should feel okay about pursuing money, but we also should be making sure it flows. The whole point is to keep prosperity flowing to everyone.*
A. Sounds good.

Q. *I answered my own question didn't I? (Laughter)*
A. Yes. At this stage we are just focusing on establishing the view of inherent wealth, which is the basis of the wealthy outlook you

are talking about. But I would say that is a universal principle of enlightened economy.

Buddhism has a lot to say about generosity and there is that kind of encouragement to partner with others, regardless of faith, in Islam and Judaism and other religions as well. But for this series of talks we're just focusing on the view, because it's the foundation of everything.

Q2. *I actually have a hard time putting one definition on such things as monetary wealth, emotional wealth, intellectual wealth and so forth. In my mind those are totally different boxes. I was thinking that there are very bitter poor people and very bitter rich people. There are really happy poor people and really happy rich people. There is no such thing as a rich household or poor household, no such thing. It just depends on how hard you look. You can't make broad statements like "All rich people are..."*

I was thinking, maybe there is an equation that somehow connects the amount of money we possess with our emotional and intellectual capacity to digest it and to work with our needs. If there are needs, then maybe there is an amount of money that will meet them. If the amount of money we have is much lower than our intellectual and emotional needs, then we won't be happy.

A. There is an expression "joining heaven and earth," which refers to the uniquely human potential to join vision with practical reality. We have that capacity, but when heaven and earth don't connect it creates frustration. Often it's because we have not made a relationship with where we are, or we don't respect who or where we are as a legitimate starting place. We feel that it's a copout to accept where we are as good ground. We think we need an explanation or a scapegoat for why we're here when we "shouldn't be". Sometimes the problem is not having a vision big enough to inspire us.

But from the Buddhist point of view, right where we are is basically good. There are a million reasons why we are where we are at any stage in our lives, so we have to start by appreciating "here" and then go forward. Otherwise, if you start with a chip on your shoulder or with some kind of impetuous agenda, you're perpetuating the sense of struggle. It's still trying to manipulate what's out there without first making the connection between the outside projections and the inside projector.

That is not to say one shouldn't relate to the outside world; just don't relate to the outside world from the point of view of poverty mentality. You can afford to take your seat, respect wherever you are, as the first step to moving forward. That's actually a very generous way to be, because you can also see others more completely. You can relate with someone else because you are not preoccupied by being stuck in your self-imagined cell, banging against those walls. It's not necessary to do that. Does that make sense?

> *You can afford to take your seat,*
> *respect wherever you are, as the*
> *first step to moving forward.*

Q2. *Yes, in a way it does, but some places are definitely not good to stay. If you come home and your house is closed and you have no food and all of a sudden you have no clothing...*
A. That's a good point. That is an example of connecting with the practical realities of a situation, which is the "earth" aspect. To be sure, some situations are very extreme and demand a quick decision with little to go on. Whether it's clear or murky, at some point you must go with your best take. The challenge is to do that without becoming aggressive or closing down to the feedback.

I signed a 3 year lease on a cramped and poorly lit room once. It was my first apartment after graduating from college. I had been practicing meditation for two years and I thought, "I should be able to transform any place into a palace internally, if not externally" and "I should be able to be cheerful even in this dark, dingy room that costs way too much money." I tried that for a while, but I couldn't overcome the external situation. It was too much for me. I was becoming depressed. I had the vision of creating an uplifted living situation, but I failed to appreciate the earth of my own strengths and weaknesses vis-à-vis such a challenging space.

Then an old friend came along and said, "You look depressed. Why don't you move in with us here?" It was a nice room in a house with big windows, no lease required, and cheaper rent. But I felt like that would be cheating—I wouldn't even consider it.

Then someone with more perspective on the rental market convinced me that I was in an unreasonable situation and that I could and should break the lease (forfeiting two months' rent). I felt guilty and embarrassed about my hypocrisy, but over time I realized that was one of those situations where I had gone too far. Only when my perspective had expanded was it possible to make a fresh start—but only if I accepted myself honestly and trusted my intelligence over my logic.

Joining heaven and earth begins with a vast vision like creating enlightened society. Then you bring that down a bit to something more immediately workable, like a wonderful place to live and entertain friends. Finally, you try to perk up your surroundings whatever they may be as your ground. Sakyong Mipham discusses joining heaven and earth in detail in the book, *Ruling Your World*.

So you work on your external situation like we've done in our meditation hall. We've created a situation that's decent, as much as we can, as much as our budget will allow. It's an ongoing process. When we come in here to sit (meditate), sometimes there are obstacles that come up: people talking outside, noises down the street...but we work with those. Those are workable. And that's the point. You take your external situation to the point where you can, and then you work with the rest internally. It's a balanced approach between internal and external; you're not rejecting or ignoring anything.

Q3. *(Assistant Teacher) When you were talking about the room, the concept of fixed mind came up for me. Someone once told me, "You have to stop 'shoulding' on yourself," sort of a pun. But that's fixed mind when you go, "This is what I have to do, this is what I should do..." It's like this voice, that's maybe not even yours, saying, "I should be able to live here, I should be able to work it out." It's a trap of fixed mind. Life is a fluid thing, which is sort of uncertain, but also totally open. I've had the trap of fixed mind and suffered. I did some of my best suffering (laughter) in that state of dumb ignorance, that animal realm.*

A. I think the first thing you do is you lean into it a little bit, because we are all in boxes like that in our lives, all the time. Like when you are on the meditation cushion and you've got some pain, you lean into that a little bit and see how that works, but then sometimes it's too big of a distraction and you need to make a change, so you have to change your position for a while and then try again.

I've given you a rather philosophical discussion tonight, but the approach of meditation is to work with your life from the point of view of perspective, just widening your perspective. So it's not so much about manipulating. Meditation is the alternative to that. Normally we try to work with the external situation, and we are going to do that; but what meditation allows us to do and what the vehicle of meditation is really about, is creating a broader understanding of the internal and external dimensions by simply expanding awareness. Then the best decisions reveal themselves.

If we take the example of the rooming house, I just didn't know. I was in my early 20s. I didn't know what was a good situation to be in. I just took the first place I could find, subject to an immature set of parameters. Then as I learned more about what was going on, internally as well as externally, I allowed myself to consider more options. In that case it made sense to go another way. Expanding perception as much as you can is the ideal way to approach every tough decision. At some point you have to go with what you've got, take a leap. If you remain open to the feedback, your perception will expand again based on that.

Thank you.

Expanding perception as much as you can is the ideal way to approach every tough decision.

The First Noble Truth of Wealth

The introductory talk I gave last week was entitled "Inherent Wealth: Discovering Richness in Yourself and in Your World." We began by examining how we look for wealth in our lives, how we have been operating with respect to making our lives richer, and how that hasn't quite worked.

The way we define wealth is very significant in terms of how it affects our world. Conventional definitions of wealth haven't been very satisfying. So it's very helpful and important to examine the nature of wealth because it drives a lot of emotions and decision-making.

When I was a kid, I was very excited about digging a hole to China with my friends. When it turned out to be slow going, we figured we probably just hadn't dug deep enough. Most of us are accustomed to seeking wealth in a similarly naive way. The presumption is that if we could just bring in a little more of the things that we associate with wealth like money or power, the right job or relationship...then we would also get what we really want, which could be called "wealthiness." Upon closer examination, our relationship with wealth has been mostly about hurdles; self-imposed pre-requisites to a wealthy state of mind.

You might think money is a good proxy for wealth, but the value of money is relative. How much money do you want? How much money do you need? My experience is that if I have one dollar, I need two dollars; if I have ten thousand, I want twenty thousand. Because whenever you arrive at one place, there is always something that needs to be fixed, taxes that need to be paid, something desirable that is just out of reach. So the wealthiness that any amount of money brings is very dependent on mind.

The wealthiness that any amount of money brings is very dependent on mind.

From the Buddhist perspective it is possible to approach wealth more directly. The reason that we have been pursuing wealth indirectly, through money for example, is because it is easy to measure and meet basic needs with it, which has obvious value. "Wealthiness" on the other hand is not so easy to measure, much less bank. It's a state of mind, and everybody knows that a state of mind is not a solid thing. A state of mind is also something we can create for ourselves, so that is cheating right? Nevertheless, there's no point in accumulating stuff if you don't end up granting yourself that feeling. So why wait?

The way to make a connection with genuine wealth begins with taking responsibility for one's own state of mind.

The view of inherent wealth is that wealth is already present within us and around us. It is that wealthiness and wealthy outlook are completely up to us. Flipping that around we could say that wealthiness is entirely our own responsibility. The way to make a connection with genuine wealth begins with taking responsibility for one's own state of mind.

The First Noble Truth (of Wealth)

The Four Noble Truths is a traditional Buddhist teaching. It is one of the first teachings that the Buddha gave. It is frequently offered at the beginning stage of teachings because it pretty well summarizes the spiritual path.

The Four Noble Truths are traditionally contemplated in pairs. The first two are:

I.   The Truth of Suffering
II. The Cause of Suffering

And the second two are:

III. The Cessation of Suffering
IV. The Path

Tonight's talk is on The Truth of Suffering so it is designed to deflate you. *(Laughter)* It feels like I should apologize for that or something, but in reality, recognizing the common ground of the human condition is a huge relief and one of the greatest insights one can ever discover.

What I mean by The Four Noble Truths of Wealth is that I am presenting the traditional Four Noble Truths, but with examples from economic life. So it is a traditional teaching presented in the context of the challenges and opportunities we all have with money and livelihood.

The First Noble Truth is The Truth of Suffering. You could say that life, including economic life, is suffering by it's very nature. That is a controversial thing to say. Some people will embrace it immediately, maybe a little too quickly, and some people will think it's a pessimistic outlook. Either way, suffering in this context is connected to fear, fear of change, fear of pain, fear of sadness, which I find especially interesting.

The very first teaching the Buddha gave was that life is characterized by universal impermanence. The uncertainty of impermanence invites fear. If you think about it, all frustration, anxiety, ignorance, aggression, and desperation boils down to fear—and ultimately, all fears stem from the fear of death.

The very first teaching the Buddha gave was that life is characterized by universal impermanence.

You could say that death is an analogy for anything unknown, and that the unknown is analogous to death. So death is the big impermanence and the foundation of all fear.

Traditionally fear is subcategorized into two types. The first type is *fear of losing what is precious to you.* We have certain people, relationships, comforts, and even ideas that are precious to us, and we are afraid to lose those.

This could be as simple as fear you'll be late for your lunch date, or as profound as fear of losing a loved one.

The second type of fear is *fear of getting what you don't want.* It could be fear of catching the flu or fear of being attacked, fear of being audited on your taxes. It has a way of expanding into fear of being in any circumstances that are outside of your control.

The Misery of Economic Life

In economic life, fear is always with us, no question about it. Why is that? Fundamentally, it's because of impermanence. Impermanence simply means that everything that comes together (i.e. everything), without exception, eventually comes apart. That makes life stressful, especially if you try to eliminate it or ignore it.

In economic life, fear is always with us, no question about it.

Impermanence is readily observable in economics. The economy and any business within it are cyclical and dynamic. Business is competitive. Employment is unpredictable, and almost by definition, a good job is hard to get. Then, when you finally get a good job, it turns out to have politics. Anything that people care about has politics, and clearly, the more people care about it, the more politics there are.

Anything that people care about has politics, and clearly, the more people care about it, the more politics there are.

So you might find a great job with a wonderful non-profit organization that helps people in great need, and then discover that it is a treacherous swamp of jealousy and back-biting—all because people care so much about what they are doing that they are keenly interested in how it gets done. There's always tension, because people have different perspectives.

Employment also means uncertainty, because along with a job comes the possibility that you could lose that job. Even if you do have that dream job, you may get promoted, or transferred, or given responsibilities that are stressful for you.

You can live with that, and you can learn to be careful about working with other people's feelings. Even though you may be very skillful, office politics and uncertainty are always there to be managed. Even if you do manage things well, circumstances can change—they are impermanent.

You could try to escape office politics through self-employment, but as those of us who are self-employed have learned, that simply means moving the politics home! So you actually didn't get rid of the politics, you just now have the politics with your spouse or whomever you live with, customers, business partners, suppliers, and employees. The good news is that self-employment is physically, mentally, and financially all consuming, and highly unlikely to succeed.

The good news is that self-employment is physically, mentally, and financially all consuming, and highly unlikely to succeed.

Once you get past the humiliation, unemployment can be spacious, suddenly having all that time on your hands. But job hunting is a rollercoaster of hope and fear as the clock ticks down on your savings and support system. Sooner or later the benefits run out and you are keenly aware of your dependence on your spouse, your family, or worse, the state. Welfare is a bitch.

Underemployment is almost not worth mentioning because I've never met anyone that wasn't. It could be that underemployment

is underrated except for the low pay, odd hours, tyrannical managers, and small-minded co-workers. Apart from that, it's great.

Whether you work for yourself or for someone else, ironically,
the most common goal of working people is retiring. Maybe you
would even like to achieve early retirement. So you set a goal: "If
I can just get X amount of money..." You try to save your money
and you tell yourself you are just sweating it out in this miserable
job because there is a pension. You hang in there day after day,
year after year, and commiserate with your co-workers how dread-
ful the work environment is. But you are all miserable together,
waiting for that pension to be there for you. In the meantime, all
you can do is secretly hope your boss will get sacked, promoted,
or transferred so you can move up, or anywhere but here.

---

*Ironically, the most common goal
of working people is retiring.*

When the day comes to retire, the retirement party is anti-
climactic, to say the least, and it turns out that the pension wasn't
quite what you thought. You actually miss being miserable/needed
at the office. Your spouse drives you nuts at home all day long and
you find that you are quite hurt that the people at the office are
just picking up and moving on without you after all those years
together. They miss you in the morning, but then they're plan-
ning where to go for lunch. It turns out you were valuable, but
replaceable, and that's a painful thing to realize.

My father was a sociology professor. He loved his work so much
that my mother was concerned for many years that he would never
retire, that he would want to work 'til kingdom come. My mother
worked 9–5 as a school psychologist and she looked forward to
retirement very much.

Unexpectedly, my father received a moral ultimatum, so to speak, from his university. The dean asked if he would take an early retirement package, telling him, 'if you stay on, we have to let these two junior professors go.' My dad was hurt by being confronted with such a dilemma. He had to choose between early retirement from a job he loved or to stay on at the expense of two younger professors whom he had probably recruited and mentored. So he ended-up retiring a year or two before my mother.

Surprisingly, my father retired fairly easily, I think because the lifestyle of a professor is very self-managed. You have control of your time. You are very self-reliant, and people come and go often. He missed many things about his job, but the contrast between his days of work and days of retirement was not so cut and dry. He just continued reading and researching things.

Ironically, it was my mother with the 9–5 job who had a hard time with the retirement transition, even though she had been looking forward to it quite a bit.

When I was an investment advisor, I had clients with great work ethics and big plans for retirement with a Winnebago or something. Some of them died very soon after retirement. You couldn't help but wonder if it was because retirement was a meaningless vacuum versus the fulfilling engagement their working lives had offered. Who knew?

You couldn't help but wonder if it was
because retirement was a meaningless
vacuum versus the fulfilling engagement their
working lives had offered. Who knew?

So we have employment, which looks good to begin with, but is often painful in various ways. We have self-employment, which has its ups and downs. And we have retirement, which is often a hollow victory. We are all working toward it, in one form or another, day in and day out, but retirement is also no slam-dunk to happiness. All of these things have meaningful sides, but they are not the final solutions to our anxiety we hope for.

Finally, there's inheritance (or any large windfall). Sometimes we think, "Gee, maybe I'm going to inherit big money and everything is going to change." Depending on where the projected inheritance is in the scheme of things, we give up in subtle ways and start coasting. We make a lot of odd decisions in our lives based upon the expectation of inheritance.

But the inheritance often doesn't materialize when we expect it to, and we find ourselves in this weird moral place anticipating it while trying to abstract that from wishing for the demise of a loved one. Then, you might actually get the inheritance and discover that the loss of your benefactor comes with a feeling of emptiness and re-focused anxiety about your own mortality.

Even if you know exactly how much your inheritance is going to be, it never goes according to plan. Inheritance, or any windfall for that matter, is usually anti-climactic. It doesn't create a permanent state of wealthiness. It's just one more prop and you find there is more work to be done. You haven't even begun to figure out what will make you *feel* wealthy.

Even if you know exactly how much
your inheritance is going to be, it
never goes according to plan.

When I was a stockbroker I had many clients who burned through their inheritance trying to maintain a lifestyle, or speculating in the financial markets like big shots at a poker table. They were trying to rationalize the windfall by "earning it" again. It was a common syndrome. You got the feeling that maybe they had to burn through it as part of their journey to maturity.

So inheritance can be an obstacle, from a spiritual point of view. An inheritance could set you back, distract you from discovering more unconditional wealth.

All told, economic life is inherently painful. There it is. I told you this talk was depressing! We could go further and talk about how much money it would take to "get rich." But whatever form of wealth, whatever amount you have, if you have any kind of a creative mind, it's very easy to find it insufficient. Ultimately, external wealth is really only of use to the extent that it helps you feel wealthy; and there are more direct ways to approach that.

So The First Noble Truth of wealth is that life, including economic life, is characterized by pain and suffering due to constant uncertainty, which invokes fear. A subtle form of fear pervades life. There is impermanence. There is no safe haven. There is no easy answer. Whatever position we build up against fear will crumble.

Fear can be exhilarating or the vanguard of suffering depending upon whether we let it lead to panic. The first part of fear is heightened awareness. Panic is when we shut the information gathering down, which leads to ignoring things and bad affirmations. Panic invites us to solidify our worst-case projections, which rationalize quick and dirty solutions. That's why we need to make a better relationship with fear. Life may be inherently painful, but it is made far more painful by attempting to ignore fear or regarding fear and pain as failures. Like pain, fear is natural. It's how we relate with pain and fear that's interesting.

The traditional Buddhist analogy for fear turning into panic is "mistaking a rope for a snake." If you wake up in the middle of the night and see a rope on your bedroom floor, you might panic and think, "It's a snake!" Imagine how a little assumption like that could influence your activity over the next few seconds, most of which would not be good. But then if you look a little longer or turn on a light, you will see that the snake is, in fact, just a rope.

Fear can be exhilarating or the vanguard of suffering depending upon whether we let it lead to panic.

That is the relationship between fear and panic. Panic is the reaction to fear that shuts off the information flow and runs away with whatever superficial data you've got. It invites the most defensive interpretation of events and often the most counterproductive solutions. If you convince yourself you are out of your depth, you can drown in shallow water. We react differently when we are panicked, on a large or small scale. You could say fear is just a feeling of uncertainty and panic is when fear becomes rationalized by its own assumptions. That is the moment when your world becomes solidified and unworkable. Panic is a premature grasp for certainty that is based on defensive projections instead of open absorption.

Panic is the reaction to fear that shuts off the information flow and runs away with whatever superficial data you've got.

My first meditation instructor once told me, "Rest in panic," meaning don't buy into it. Make friends with your fear, be curious about it, try to hang out with it as long as you can. Resist freaking out. A lot of information comes in during that split second of time between fear and panic. In Shambhala we call that "holding your seat." It's extraordinarily beneficial.

Although we fear pain as a proxy of death, it is equally emblematic of life. In the modern world we don't contemplate death; but rather avoid all pain indiscriminately as a paranoid pre-emptive measure, a microcosm of avoiding death. Sometimes I think our greatest fear is not death but sadness, and we fear death so much because we're afraid sadness will come with it.

Although we fear pain as a proxy of death, it is equally emblematic of life.

Fear and Pain

If we can slow down enough to withstand our fear a little, it's possible to explore pain. Pain can be broken down. We should be more curious about pain, because a simplistic relationship to pain creates a whole lot more pain, which is the bulk of our suffering. Instead of fearing pain wholesale, we could even become connoisseurs of its different vintages. Sounds kinky, I know.

We tend to judge our experience in terms of "what's good for me" and "what's not so good for me." But that is a very quantitative or linear approach to life: more pain vs. less pain. If you really look at your experience, you will find that pain, every pain, is a unique, self-described experience. It has qualitative aspects we can afford to explore. If this pain had a color what would it be? How deep is it? Is it psychological or physical or both? What's the relationship? Where exactly is it located? What role does it play? Is it permanent? What information comes with it? Where does it originate? And when you really look at it, is it really pain or is it just prickly? Sometimes pain is mixed with pleasure or just direct feedback, which can be a real gift at times.

If you really look at your experience,
you will find that pain, every pain, is
a unique, self-described experience.

We effectively relate to pain as if it is just one bad thing because we are so mentally speedy, but there are many different types—heartbreak, longing, worry, concern, heat, cold, aches and itches, failure, vanity... We would do anything to avoid having our hearts broken for instance. And yet the experience of heartbreak can be rich and beautiful and the source of genuine empathy.

If you can appreciate a heroic tragedy or good blues, you can appreciate that heartbreak actually has a quality of renewal. You can come out of incredibly heartbreaking situations, whether it's the loss of a job or the love of your life, and still find humor and relief because such catastrophes also create a lot of space to breathe.

We're inclined to assume that uncertainty is the harbinger of pain and therefore bad. But it begs the question: how can one experience true joy or friendship if one is not prepared to expose one's heart?

Dodging vulnerability keeps us from making a wholehearted relationship with others. This is sometimes called "neurotic speed." We want to avoid pain so much that we habitually run away from it, even though in many cases just letting things be uncomfortable for a while may be the best solution. Holding one's seat can turn a snake back into a rope or maybe just a garter snake, like your partner or boss. Maybe he or she is afraid too.

It may be possible to look more closely at fear if we are more curious about pain. We have a great deal more capacity to be

vulnerable than we think. A lot of the aggression and related suffering that goes on in the world stems from someone's rationalization that they are in pain, or they are threatened with pain; and
therefore can justify all kinds of "pre-emptive" aggressive actions
and collateral damage.

*We have a great deal more capacity
to be vulnerable than we think.*

When the United States became threatened by the remote
possibility of WMD in Iraq. The government rationalized fear into
panic and mounted a war based on the weakest evidence. How
easy it was for a whole country to turn a garter snake into a cobra,
based on fear alone. If we allow that type of reaction to prevail,
soon we will have killed every bee, shark, spider...everything in the
world with the remotest chance of biting us—including each other.

*The pain and the learning
process are closely related.*

Pain has a role to play in business as well. Part of my job is
to train mortgage brokers. When a new agent loses a deal, it's
often because they have not developed their skills yet or because
a competing bank has the power to take a loss to win the deal. It
is extremely discouraging to have that experience but it is in the
nature of any business to go through that occasionally (or quite
often). That is a perspective one only gains from enduring a number
of painful experiences. For a new person it's heartbreaking because

they haven't had the benefit of all those painful experiences to put things into a larger perspective. They have a lot of hope and fear invested in their first few deals. They're trying to do a great job. This situation is true in many walks of life, being a beginner is painful. You'd like to help them avoid all those disappointments, but the pain and the learning process are closely related.

The Three Kinds of Pain

The pain of human life is traditionally broken down into three categories.

The first category is **the pain of alternation**, which is simply that things don't always go the way we want them to go. We are not saying anything big here, just that things don't always work out. Sometimes they do, which makes us hopeful, and sometimes they don't, which makes us fearful, or is it the other way around? Either way, the alternation between these two is painful—but natural. There is progress and then there is disappointment. We have the pain of alternation in business all the time, and we have it throughout life i.e. stop expecting it to go away!

The second category is **the pain of pain**, which could be called pain squared. Because when dogs are down, they frequently do get kicked, or in the case of humans, they kick themselves. Anybody who has gone through school knows that if you are lonely or depressed, you might attract a bully—because you are down! In the business world, if your company is losing money, another company might take it over and kick you out. If your sales commissions go down, you might also lose your job. If the bank finds out you lost your job, they might cancel your low interest line of credit.

Or there's embarrassment. You might feel like you should be doing better; so you beat yourself up because you've got some difficulties that other people might see. You give yourself a hard time on top of the original pain, because you think people are not supposed to be in pain. If you have a bankruptcy, that can happen. You punish yourself for having taken a punishment. You feel like you should have somehow avoided that, that you were never supposed to have the experience of failure or pain.

You give yourself a hard time on top of the original pain, because you think people are not supposed to be in pain.

There are many schools of thought that say our projections onto our world have the power to create our circumstances through the "law of attraction" and other means. I think that is probably true in more ways than we expect, but we must be careful not to fall into a strategic approach, which constructs rather than dismantles superstitions. For example a wealthy outlook is different than delusions of grandeur. One is based on unconditional appreciation, the other on escapism. Also, if we become confused between the cause and the appearance of poverty for example, we might never discover the roots of our own or someone else's hard time, for fear we might be "attracting" more trouble.

That is another example of the pain of pain. When we meet somebody who is in a great deal of pain it can be very hard to relate to him or her properly. Maybe that is partially because it's just a little too close to home. The closer you get, the easier it is to identify with them and you see how it could easily happen to you!

This may be the whole point of strategies that advocate manipulating what to think about, on the basis that whatever you think of most will eventually be "attracted". But that is a defensive approach. Pushing thoughts away and obsessing over them are two sides of the same coin. With a little mind training, we can afford to be curious about pain without becoming obsessed with it. I don't think nurses and doctors and parents are worse off for doing so. That kind of bravery is what makes us strong, spiritually at least.

So, instead of being frightened of our own minds, we should be more inquisitive and engender a positive outlook without attempting to manipulate our thoughts in hope to dodge fear. It's counterproductive because that kind of strategy is a form of panic itself.

The spiritual approach is to encourage curiosity about fear and ultimately to regard whatever threat comes into your life as an opportunity to develop fearlessness through insight vs. tactics. The way to begin is always to work with whatever is in front of us. The problem is when we reject where we are because right where we are is always our ideal starting place. Our ultimate opportunity is always what's in front of us. Whatever our challenges are right now, there's a lot of information in them and so they are also our chances to develop wisdom and humor and virtue.

> *Our ultimate opportunity is always what's in front of us.*

So there is the pain of alternation, the pain of pain, and last but not least is **all-pervasive pain**.

It is said that only the Buddhas can recognize all-pervasive pain. *Buddha* means one who is fully awake, so I am taking a big leap here, but I think all-pervasive pain has to do with the pain of duality. It is the all-pervasive pain of being in the state of believing one is separate from and independent of the world, which leads us through life bewildered and frustrated like a bull in a china shop.

One analogy that is given for all-pervasive pain is that the way you and I would experience a hair on the palm of the hand is like a hair in the eye for a Buddha. The idea is that the more awake you are, the more sensitive you are. It's important to understand that, because the more you become tuned in to your world, the more sensitive and vulnerable and heart broken you become. That kind of humility is actually a good thing because it is the gateway to wisdom and confidence and joy.

---

*The idea is that the more awake you
are, the more sensitive you are.*

As you walk the spiritual path, the subtlety of your awareness might increase, and an increase in awareness is also an increase in vulnerability, and that's fine. The spiritual path is actually a process of opening ourselves up to being touched by the world on more and more subtle levels, and so we become more sensitive as a result.

So The First Noble Truth is that life is inherently painful, and life, we could say, is suffering. But we can make the distinction that suffering comes from our denial of life's inherent pain. Suffering is the huge amount of extra pain that comes from not acknowledging fear. It's the years of angst and defensive negativity you spend in fear of losing your job vs. the mix of pain and relief on the day you actually lose it.

Meditation practice is the vehicle we use to make a relationship with things as they are, even though things are sometimes painful. Through the practice of sitting meditation we are training ourselves not to judge our experience so quickly. We can afford to feel what we feel without reacting defensively or adventitiously toward it.

When you sit down on the meditation cushion, you are training yourself to be present even in the face of insecurity. Fear drives us to react to uncertainty with a storyline and strategy. If somebody says something in an odd tone or looks at us the wrong way, we start to ask ourselves, "What was that for? Why did he do that?

Was there something wrong with me? Are my ears too big? Who does she think she is? Does my nose look funny?" That's all fine if we can let that uncertainty be there without solidifying it.

When you sit down on the meditation cushion, you are training yourself to be present even in the face of insecurity.

Meditation is sometimes analogous to parachuting, because when we follow the technique, we are learning to let go of our thoughts without a replacement plan. We are training ourselves not to react to fear, or its vanguard—boredom, habitually. Just let uncertainty be and see what happens.

The Second Noble Truth of Wealth

This talk was preceded by the group meditation instruction in Appendix A.

The introductory talk in this series was entitled "Inherent Wealth: Discovering Richness in Yourself and in Your World." In that talk we discussed how the way we define wealth is very significant in our world, because so much of our society and experience is organized around that.

We explored further how wealth is illusive. For most people a sense of wealthiness is not particularly reliable. The reason for that may be that the way we've been approaching it—externally—is actually pursuing wealth indirectly. Nobody wants external wealth for its own sake in the end; it's the way we presume more money will make us feel that we are actually interested in.

The assumption is that if we accumulate external wealth, we will be able to use it to feel wealthy. That seems pretty straightforward, because there is obvious value in wealth by external measures. However, given that external wealth and a sense of wealthiness have both proven to be so unattainable and/or unreliable with the outside in approach, maybe it's time to try focusing less on what we have or haven't got and more on how we feel since that is the key outcome anyway. It may be more viable to explore the feeling of wealthiness and assume that material wealth will be easier to work with for having done that.

Maybe it's time to try focusing less on what we have or haven't got and more on how we feel since that is the key outcome anyway.

So seeking financial or material wealth is not actually pursuing wealthiness directly. If we want to "pursue" wealthiness more directly we should cultivate a wealthy outlook, but we don't really know how to do that in a sustainable way. There is a tendency to think we need more. But that's an endless quest because wealthiness is more than an external circumstance; King Midas is an example of that; he was granted his wish that everything he touched would turn to gold, but then he touched someone he loved by mistake.

The idea of defining wealth experientially is interesting, and it's also interesting to think about how our society would organically transform over time if we all understood wealth more completely and approached it more directly.

The Buddhist view is that wealthiness is a reflection of expansive awareness. Inseparable from enlightenment, the essence of wealth is inherent and natural to human beings. So it's not a matter of pursuing wealth, but removing obstructions to perceiving it internally and externally. In fact, it becomes a little unclear what's internal and external because ultimately, wealth is always a matter of perception.

The Buddhist view is that wealthiness is a reflection of expansive awareness.

The economist Milton Friedman once said, "Inflation is always and everywhere a monetary phenomenon." As Buddhist economists, we can say that wealth is always and everywhere a matter of perception.

As Buddhist economists, we can say that wealth is always and everywhere a matter of perception.

Understanding that wealth is always perception makes it possible to have a better relationship with it. If wealth is perception then the capacity for it is inherent to being human. Recognizing that materialism is not the only way to work with wealth, we needn't restrict ourselves with such high hopes for it.

What kind of a society might evolve out of the assumption that wealth is inherent? It's wonderful to imagine what might happen if we all started to make decisions from a wealthy point of view. Communication and creativity would definitely increase.

The journey of inherent wealth begins with the view. It is to thoroughly explore the internal understanding of wealth, which might be a more accurate one. We have to examine this alternative way of looking at things systematically, experience it fully for ourselves. Only then will our allegiance naturally switch to it. Otherwise it's just another philosophical production.

So we have to ask ourselves what's missing from the way we've been thinking? What is the source of the issues that we have? And what is the alternative? Having done that kind of research, we can realize wealth that arises more from insight than from habitual pursuit patterns.

Through meditation practice and examining our experience, we can learn to use the ordinary disciplines and activities of life to help us discover and maintain a deeper sense of well-being.

Most of us have tried to jump into arts and disciplines from kickboxing to crochet and discovered that personal discipline makes us feel good. But if personal discipline or virtue alone were enough, every accomplished executive or selfless caretaker would be cheerful as the Buddha. Sadly that is not the case. Without a thorough grounding in the view, the benefits of external and even psychological disciplines will be limited. Consequently, when you fall off the exercise diet or philosophical horse, when you have a bad day, it's harder to get back on because you haven't invested the time and effort to get to know yourself at the foundation level.

If personal discipline or virtue alone were enough, every accomplished executive or selfless caretaker would be cheerful as the Buddha. Sadly that is not the case.

When we have made friends with ourselves unconditionally we can apply that same goodwill in our relationships with others as well.

The Buddhist way of helping others is from the inside out, starting with one. It's hard to help anyone in a lasting sense unless we have discovered a wealthy outlook ourselves. Without that we tend to think we are giving a handout, which is mutually confusing. Alternatively, a wealthy outlook is the source of limitless energy to extend ourselves to others without condescension.

We still have challenges in daily life to deal with, of course. Work, relationships, money—all those things must be respected. But if you don't know how to genuinely cheer yourself up, success can even be an obstacle to wealthiness because it can be distracting.

*If you don't know how to genuinely cheer
yourself up, success can even be an obstacle
to wealthiness because it can be distracting.*

Beyond the level of basic needs, increases in income are beneficial only if used to create balance and wisdom. Money is really just a resource like water or a vitamin that can be very helpful if used wisely, but it is not health itself, it is not the ultimate goal. A glass of water several times a day is very helpful; a gallon all at once? Not so much.

At very low levels of income, money may be very closely associated with wealth, but there is a bigger point of view.

The talk preceding this one was called The First Noble Truth of Wealth. The First Noble Truth is that life is suffering. Suffering in this sense is characterized by fear. You could say fear is ultimately fear of pain, the ultimate pain is presumed to be death. So suffering is ultimately based on the fear of death.

We normally conduct ourselves in ignorance and de facto denial of death despite the fact that everything we know and experience has a temporary quality, including our notion of who we are. Everything that comes together has a lifespan. So, by nature, death is at the end of every situation, every relationship, and every thing.

*We normally conduct ourselves in
ignorance and de facto denial of death
despite the fact that everything we know
and experience has a temporary quality,
including our notion of who we are.*

The message of The First Noble Truth is that by acknowledging the presence of impermanence, fear and suffering, it is possible to examine our experience more closely. It is quite daring to look at it even though we are afraid of what we might see.

Fear is traditionally broken down into two categories:

1. *Fear of losing what is dear to us.* This could be situations, relationships. It could be our own life, body, health, or sense of security; it could also be one's own self-image.

2. *Fear of getting what we don't want.* This includes getting the wrong kind of attention in various ways like from the tax auditor, being hacked, attacked, contracting a disease or just getting into trouble—when things go the wrong way.

Fear and suffering are associated with the struggle to avoid pain and traditionally there are three categories of pain.

The first kind of pain is **the pain of alternation.** Sometimes things go our way and sometimes they don't. Or sometimes life is going really well and then it goes quite the other way. Sometimes you have the fiercest arguments with your spouse right when you have been getting along famously. You've built up great expectations and then you feel so betrayed when you rediscover that your partner has their own independent existence.

You can see the pain of alternation in business and economic life too. Sometimes business is easy and sometimes it's not. Sometimes you feel like you are ahead of the game. Next thing you know, you feel alone and surrounded by competition, or that your competition is so much better organized than you. Maybe you are being underestimated or misjudged.

The next kind of pain is **the pain of pain.** When you have some pain, you frequently get more pain. Your business is not doing so well, and then, because your volume is down your suppliers charge you more and threaten to cut you off. Your income goes down and on top of that your spouse is unhappy because you're not pulling your weight.

So the pain of pain is simply that a dog gets kicked when he's down—or kicks himself for being down. You see that in finance all the time. The more desperately you need a loan, the harder it is to qualify and the more it might cost when you do. Or in another form, we feel ashamed or embarrassed that we are having pain. You are late following up a lead and so you are afraid to make the call, and then you give yourself a hard time for having lost the deal even before you have lost it because it was your own fault. Everyone feels this in one way or another.

The third and last kind of pain is called **all-pervasive pain**. It's been said that only Buddhas can feel all-pervasive pain, a very subtle form of pain associated with the notion of duality. The fact that we experience our lives in the form of duality at all is very painful.

You could say that just taking form, becoming attached to an aging body, is so far from how things could be if one were completely free of egotistical concerns, it is miserable. Being surrounded by profound ignorance and unnecessary suffering must be incredibly painful to one who knows better like an optimist working in an office where everyone habitually gripes about the morale problem. We usually don't recognize how we perpetuate our own suffering because we can't imagine anything other than an egocentric way of looking at things. From the Buddhist point of view such ignorance leads to suffering, not bliss.

We usually don't recognize how we perpetuate our own suffering because we can't imagine anything other than an egocentric way of looking at things.

If we acknowledge that life is painful by nature, we could develop some curiosity about pain. A great deal of suffering and fear stems from habitually operating in denial that life is temporary and that it is painful. Every moment is precious and fleeting at the same time. Much difficulty, aggression, and "out-of-sync-ness" occur in our lives because we ignore or deny this basic reality. Think about how the world would be if everybody remembered that we are all going to be dead in 50 years give or take *(laughs)*. We might be a little more easygoing.

The Second Noble Truth (of Wealth)

The Second Noble Truth is the cause or the origin of suffering.

The origin of suffering is the belief in an independent ego or self. Here ego is the belief in a static identity. From the Buddhist point of view, ego is just a convenient assumption that was made way back, or way back at the beginning of every moment. We believe we have a solid continuous ego that just popped up out of nowhere. Based on that little assumption of independent origination, we have developed a great many defensive ways of seeing the world on an egotistical basis.

> *The origin of suffering is the belief in an independent ego or self.*

The notion of a separate self creates an imaginary fortress to defend. That fortress appears constantly under attack because everything is impermanent; everything eventually crumbles. Every wall eventually comes down, including the walls of ego, which from the Buddhist point of view is simply an ever-changing product of a long stream of causes and effects. We assume that there would be no intelligence or motivation without ego, when in fact ego is more like anti-virus software that corrupts our data and clogs up our CPU all by itself. So the mistaken ideal of a continuous identity sets up a self-perpetuating maintenance problem.

We assume that there would be no intelligence or motivation without ego, when in fact ego is more like anti-virus software that corrupts our data and clogs up our CPU all by itself.

The conventional approach to all of this is to shore up a really strong fortress! Maybe you can even smooth out the walls to make your you-ness look formidable. If you want to make your fortress really strong, you put steel rebar inside of the cement, in the form of some kind of spiritual practice or philosophical rationale in support of your extraordinary being. So then you have the illusion of fortified strength. "Come and get me now impermanence!". Because you rationalize or re-interpret every rainbow or gust of wind like it's a conceptual message, a cosmic commentary on your morality especially for you. But such superstitious psychological strategies lead into an even more confined state of internal and external image management, and create an even more conceptual relationship with all of your experience.

Our egocentric frame of reference habitually classifies everyone and every event into one of three categories: *good* in the sense that it's confirming; *bad* in the sense that it competes with whatever your goals are or offends your philosophy; and *unimportant*, or inefficient. The egocentric response to life experience is traditionally described as the three or the five poisons. The three poisons are:

neurotic passion, aggression, and ignorance. But it is said that ignorance is at the core of all three.

Neurotic speed is the glue that sustains the illusion of a solid ego. Our minds move pretty fast to avoid even acknowledging uncertainty. The defensive, egocentric outlook takes on a self-imposed urgency or arrogance because if you slow down, you start to see gaps in the wall of ego—hypocrisies between how you feel and how you are supposed to feel, for example, and that is very threatening from a solid-ego point of view. That is why meditation turns out to be so daring and so powerful. Just slowing down, the illusions of the three poisons begin to dissolve by themselves.

Neurotic speed is the glue that sustains the illusion of a solid ego.

There are two aspects or basic assumptions to the duality of having an ego. The first one is the habitual thought patterns that presume, "I need to be maintained with accomplishments or deeply held beliefs to confirm my worthiness." Your purpose in life is to get the credentials: money, relationships, degrees, and followers to re-confirm a singular distinct identity, a rationalized version of permanent success without vulnerability. There are books about how to maintain that, about how to develop a "narrative", a "personal brand," which is fraudulent by nature, of course. According to that formula, the person with the fewest gaps in their delusion of ego wins.

The second construction technique of ego's defensive view is thinking, "The outside world is solid and real i.e. independent of my own projections." If you assume that you are separate from the world, you also assume that your poverty mentality or dualistic mentality is not self-created or self-perpetuating. You are looking through blinders that block out your own role in creating every experience, so you don't see how your own attitude basically shapes your experience, including external circumstances. The ocean appears to be solid from the plane at 20,000 feet and effectively it is solid, but only because you are moving so fast. Our experience, our emotions, absolutely everything about the way we feel, is completely up to us.

The ocean appears to be solid from the plane at 20,000 feet and effectively it is solid, but only because you are moving so fast.

There are external situations that temporarily affect us. We will yell at our spouses because they are supposed to be doing things that make us feel good. Sometimes we say, "The way I feel is legitimate because this is the way I feel! Therefore, *you* must be making me feel this way!" That is an example of how ego rationalizes itself. It is the same mechanism by which fear becomes panic. The otherwise natural insecurity is fitted with logic that is customized to the situation. The accusatory mindset is so prejudicial; it brings out defensive reactions, which rationalize the accusation!

The otherwise natural insecurity is fitted with logic that is customized to the situation.

There are harder circumstances and easier circumstances to work with, to be sure, but ultimately how we feel is totally our own creation. And it's amazing what obstacles we can transform into opportunities if we resist the urge to see things defensively.

On the other hand, a positive outlook should not be confused with manipulating our own projections in order to invoke an idealized external situation. That is what my teacher called spiritual materialism. The distinction between transforming your outlook and manipulating your projections has to do with egocentricity. One expands awareness the other narrows it. One dismantles the fortress to let light shine in and out, the other tries to capture light, fence it in. One is transcendent the other is strategic. Some egotistical strategies are more sophisticated because they recognize the power of mental projections. But it is still a dualistic/materialistic approach—if you are trying to manipulate your own perception to get something else, that's a slippery slope.

Dualistic approaches advocate or at least accommodate the assumption of not being complete as you are. But from a spiritual point of view, fantasies of future riches reduce your wealthiness on the spot. Preoccupation with self-improvement introduces value judgments, which crowd out the inspiration and wisdom inherent in raw perception.

It is possible to uplift oneself with certain kinds of visualizations, but not from an egotistical point of view. The work we need to do is more about realizing our complete lack of deficiency, or you could say, realizing our unfathomable, inexhaustible inherent wealth. The objective of visualization practices in Buddhism is to help us realize the true nature of who we are already not to get somewhere else. But let's get back to the origin of suffering for now, which is fixation on the idea of a solid ego.

The work we need to do is more about realizing our complete lack of deficiency

Cocoon

Chögyam Trungpa's analogy for ego is a cocoon. The cocoon is the veil woven by the dualistic mentality, which obscures our perception. Instead of making a clear relationship with each moment, we operate from a view that is shrouded or pre-qualified behind countless assumptions and beliefs that depend on and maintain a self-image.

For example, you have your routine in the morning, like your favorite type of caffeine, or maybe your meditation practice, or whatever it might be. You regard any interruption in that to be "bad". If you didn't get a good night's sleep or a rival co-worker shows well, you might automatically assume it's a "bad" day—which becomes self-fulfilling.

When you first glimpse this cocoon, you begin to realize that whatever emotional state you are in is made of a million strands of conscious and subconscious rationalization. What did you have for dinner last night? Did you drink too much? Did you get to bed on time? How did you sleep? What time did you wake up? What did you eat in the morning? What do you have to do today? What's in front of you? And that's just within one day, maybe one hour. Then there are worlds of stuff around that like what is the story behind how you feel about your boss? It all goes into how we rationalize what we are feeling rather than experiencing each moment afresh.

You begin to realize that whatever emotional state you are in is made of a million strands of conscious and subconscious rationalization.

Unless we deliberately take a break, we have never-ending stories about ourselves and about our lives going all the time. Some of the text is on the surface, but a lot of it is much deeper—Chapter 12, or Chapter 2,000,000. "I'm not really responsible because my mom or dad was mean to me." We call that a cocoon. We all live within this web of our own storylines about who we are that are constantly unraveling and being woven again.

Another example of cocoon is seeing a spider. If you discover a spider has set down beside you, your immediate reaction is fear right? Why is that? Because one in one million spiders are mildly poisonous? Because one in a million of those might bite you? There is a better chance it will protect you from another bug with a slightly less remote chance of biting. Even though the threat is extremely remote, the spider is outside your immediate control and therefore bad or at least threatening. You must react fast to either kill it or conduct a catch and release operation, either of which puts the spider in mortal peril from you, far greater than you ever were from it. But the cocoon isn't waiting around for that perspective to get through.

Meditation practice helps us recognize that the world is not party to our highly personalized story of the universe. Because the world is operating quite independent of our expectations it often puts a little tear in the fabric of our cocoon. In through that hole come reality checks, which can feel like personal insults or bracing cold air. It comes into our smelly little cocoon and we patch it up quick with a defensive storyline. But if we flip our view and begin to understand things better, we actually come to regard that bracing air as helpful. We see that it is actually a kind of course correction, a reminder of how things really are. There is beauty, clarity, and energy in it.

The world is not party to our highly personalized story of the universe.

Living in a stuffy cocoon allows only a narrow channel of sensitivity. It is a managed existence characterized by the paranoia that accompanies obscured perception. This kind of paranoia is so common though, everyone mistakes it for normal. Anything outside of your schedule appears to get in your way, like an irritating speed bump or a threatening spider. But the world is confronting us with those all the time. The cocoon is getting punctured and worn down constantly, which keeps us madly patching it up. The idea being that we will start really living once we finally get it patched up, but this approach actually removes us further from our lives.

Through the practice of meditation we begin to see through the cocoon instead of just hiding inside it. So when we get a tear in the cocoon we might think, "Oh! That's interesting." The possibility of seeing more clearly arises and it creates the possibility of living more accurately, engaging our world more as it is. When we approach our experience without prejudgment, it's like lifting a veil, so of course there is the opportunity to make better choices. It feels very wholesome, like getting trace minerals that have been missing from one's diet.

> *Through the practice of meditation*
> *we begin to see through the cocoon*
> *instead of just hiding inside it.*

Once again, the thought patterns that make up the egotistical veil of cocoon are sometimes categorized as the three or the five poisons. The five poisons are the first three: neurotic passion, aggression, and ignorance, with the addition of pride and jealousy. But any defensive or adventitious thought pattern will do.

In the context of economic life, we have greed, which could be classified as a form of neurotic passion or wanting to control everything. Greed can manifest as the strong desire for security—wanting to stock the store room to survive a long battle against an unlimited number of foes, as imagined by ego. We will discuss aggression later, in the context of self-pity. Ignorance or narrow-mindedness about how one approaches things could just be the habit of viewing your world competitively. Pride and jealousy speak for themselves as dualistic blinders on perception of reality. All of the five poisons are gateways to what we could call poverty mentality as opposed to inherent wealth.

All of the five poisons are gateways to what we could call poverty mentality as opposed to inherent wealth.

In business, it's so easy to fall into that competitive mindset, which alternates between pride and jealousy. I was just at a business expo, and all the mortgage brokers were there. There's always an awkward moment when you meet somebody who's in your profession. "Oh hi, you're my competitor. Isn't that nice." But then you begin to realize, in reality, you're more like colleagues. Because the situation is usually much bigger than you habitually assume. Nothing shrinks your worldview like a competitive mindset. Incidentally, that's what manners and social etiquette are for, to bridge the chasm between egotistical outlook and connecting on a genuine level.

Competition in the marketplace may be helpful but ideally it reflects uplifted inspiration to serve customers and community better, like artists inspired by each other's work. Individually, a competitive mentality is at once an immediate loss of wealth and the seed of future poverty. This is true in sports as well as in business.

*Individually, a competitive mentality
is at once an immediate loss of wealth
and the seed of future poverty. This is
true in sports as well as in business.*

In my business, it's very rare that there is a truly direct competitive situation where somebody could and would take food out of your mouth—or at least it's far more rare than I frequently imagine. If somebody actually takes away your business, there could be something profoundly instructive in that. It could be that you are in the wrong market niche, but usually you just need to adjust your expectations, or tune in to the needs of your customers. Disappointment always creates a little space where fresh inspiration can come in, if you allow it.

A competitive mindset is easy to get stuck in because it self-perpetuates. It could be a form of ignorance, a narrow-minded approach, "Don't get in my way" or "your gain is my loss" kind of thinking. It is a form of egotistical defensiveness. It's a common rationale for hiding out in the narcissistic cocoon. Sometimes you see it in team members sitting at your table when you go to an industry lunch. They maintain a paranoid version of "team spirit" that feels more like an incestuous cult. Sometimes you see it in ambitious managers who micro-manage away the esprit of their team in obeisance to short-term performance measures imposed recklessly from above.

Ultimately, all actions derived from a self-centered outlook are forms of aggression. We use the word aggression in a subtle sense. The way to understand it is that the gross assumption of ego is a form of oversimplification, which results in a judgmental and inaccurate approach to life, like a frustrated bull in a china shop.

This judgmental outlook is sometimes called **poverty mentality**. The poverty mentality engendered by the five poisons is the reason why you desperately want that status object or can't stop obsessing over your bills, job search, or retirement plan. It goes beyond a balanced appreciation of something desirable. You feel you need to reinforce your existence as a separate entity by distinguishing yourself with a specific result. Ignoring the approach of death, the ultimate homogenizer, you focus on symbols at the expense of balance and heartfelt community experience. Or you just want to reassure yourself that you will live on in comfort, so you consume your lifetime projecting anxious scenarios: "What if this happens? But what if that happens? I need more buffer, this is not enough." Or I don't need any buffer because I'm an artist." Poverty mentality fritters our lives away by creating problems before they arise, makes us cut people off in traffic in a hurry to be "polite".

Ultimately, all actions derived from a self-centered outlook are forms of aggression.

At any given moment we could have a wealthy outlook that is unconditional and immediate, or we could have a poverty mentality based on the mistaken assumption that things need to be a certain way. Inside the cocoon our perception of reality is clouded by defensiveness to a greater or lesser extent depending on how central whatever it is we're working with appears to our egotistical storyline.

Poverty mentality always arises in relationship to a "self". Consciously or subconsciously, it is related to trying to protect or extend "me-ness." Under the influence of poverty mentality, if things are going well, we want to increase our "self"; maybe even use our position to get competitors into trouble.

Poverty mentality can manifest in the form of seeking more

spiritual confirmation. There are limitless layers and versions of ego e.g. trying to maintain a reputation for being "spontaneous" or "wise" for example, but all are based upon a dualistic mind-set, and therefore it is all suffering.

Poverty mentality always arises in relationship to a "self".

In *Zen Mind, Beginner's Mind* Suzuki Roshi said that the Buddha lived in a time when many traditions viewed the body as an obstacle to spirituality, a blockage to higher perception. Ascetic disciplines designed to minimize the obstacle of the body and its needs prevailed. But ultimately you can only take the body so far before you leave it, or you must recover from that, but then you are right back in it. So the ascetic approach is not sustainable, in that sense anyway.

The Buddha's discovery was that it's not the external body we have to transcend; it is the notion of duality. It is the struggle to maintain the self—we need to relax that struggle. In this sense, working with one's body is an opportunity to practice non-duality, which occurs when our body and mind are completely synchronized and connected with the environment. The aches and pains and care of one's body are also speed bumps to slow down the neurotic speed that disconnects us and opportunities to practice cheering up unconditionally.

It is the struggle to maintain the self— we need to relax that struggle.

When we are relatively new to meditation, we tend to think that through meditation practice we are going to cut through ego or get rid of it. But that can become yet another struggle. We think, "My goal is to be super-me, but without ego." My teacher's response for that kind of thinking, "You can't witness your own funeral." means that liberating oneself from ego does not feel like a personal victory. The assumption of a solid ego just becomes transparent, which feels more like a relief, a cool breeze, or taking off a heavy backpack, than a personal triumph.

The relief comes from giving up the fight for territory. It is relaxing with the holes in one's identity that creates a tremendous space for humor, curiosity, and compassion. Incidentally, you can solidify ego by pretending you have not tastes or preferences too.

It is relaxing with the holes in one's identity that creates a tremendous space for humor, curiosity, and compassion.

On the path of meditation, initially, it seems like ego needs to be uprooted like a weed in your garden. You have to pull it out by the roots. You can mow the lawn with mental or physical discipline, but the roots of ego will still be there. So from that point of view, we apply the precision of mindfulness to uproot it and pull it all out.

Further on, we say that one needs to develop awareness that sees right through the soil of our subconscious storylines, right down to the subtle roots of poverty mentality. We develop X-ray awareness vision so we can see right through to where we discover, dandelions are actually beneficial weeds on some level because they bring up nutrients for other plants.

And eventually, once we see it all, we might see it all as just the play of energy.

Start to finish, the continuity of the spiritual path is awareness. Ours is a practice of seeing. Awareness turns out to be powerful in itself, like the rays of the sun.

The last point about The Second Noble Truth is that the self-pity that accompanies the belief in a solid separate ego is the foundation rationale of aggression. I was reminded of it again tonight as I raced to get here on time. It's embarrassing to be late, especially when you are the speaker. In avoiding being late for work, you can rationalize yelling at your family. Or when your kid is waiting for you at the playground, you race through traffic with righteous fervor and put other families in danger, because at that moment you have a rock-solid rationale.

The self-pity that accompanies the belief in a solid separate ego is the foundation rationale of aggression.

Q. *So when you are late, you don't rush?*
A. Well, the point is how egocentricity is blind to its own aggression. But the example of being late means one can be brave and mature enough to face your own music. You don't have to put everyone in grave danger to solve your own problems. You may not wish to be late, but there are always tradeoffs. Hopefully your priorities are not entirely selfish. If your awareness extends beyond your own personal obsession, you see any form of aggression as counterproductive and your own reputation as increasingly expendable.

The practice of sitting meditation is our vehicle for witnessing the process of the cocoon. It is the means of seeing how each strand of habitual pattern is created, and making friends with the gaps in between them. From the relatively vast point of view of sitting meditation, we can see for the first time that our thoughts, emotions, aches and pains, are often just a reflection of insecurity with space. As meditators we relate to these psychodramas by simply bringing our awareness back to where we are—without moral judgment.

The goal of meditation is to create the simplest possible situation so that we can see how our minds operate objectively. The technique is designed to enable us to observe our mental process as clearly as possible. It's enlightening to see the process of thoughts and emotions. That's why it's extraordinarily powerful to just sit. You simply start where you are and see as much as you can. It's a bit like being an astronomer looking at the Milky Way. It is very orienting to just look and see things from a more continuous perspective. You can't see everything or even very much at one time, but gradually discover a larger understanding.

The goal of meditation is to create the simplest possible situation so that we can see how our minds operate objectively.

Q. *Would you go over what you were saying about aggression and self-pity?*
A. Nothing rationalizes aggression better than self-pity or egocentricity masquerading as the uncompromising defense of principles.

Q. *When I am sitting, I feel like I am going down, down, down to this quiet place, a deliciously quiet place. The thoughts come and go but it still feels wonderfully quiet. I love that feeling.*
A. If you look at wealth experientially, sitting meditation is actually very luxurious, because you are just completely wide open to your experience. You're actually practicing a kind of pure perception in and out. What other wealth could there be? I think the

challenge is to remain free of judgment or attachment, whatever your experience might be.

Q. *Then I thought, is this what is true nature?*
A. Meditation is definitely the best way to connect with Buddha nature, which is our inherent wakeful nature. Nevertheless, the instruction is to just touch and go. In each meditation session, there might be a peaceful quietness about it or not. But even if something else comes up, something quite different, like strong emotions, maybe that's an aspect of Buddha nature as well. The instruction is to just let that go too. That true nature, Buddha nature, basic goodness, inherent wealth, whatever you want to call it, is always there. The discipline is to just return to being completely present to discover it. It's very simple.

Q. *It's almost addictive.*
A. This is somewhat the point. We're boycotting our habit of trying to manipulate our experience, "get into the zone" all the time, because it turns out that is a convoluted way to live. With addiction there is withdrawal. Our minds are looking for something to grab onto.

The essential challenge is to be completely present and awake, just as you are, however that may be, without bias. So sounds, feelings—good or bad, everything is part of it. In my experience Buddha nature is more like crystal clarity than a bed of pillows. It's delightful, but non-dwelling. You're just right here. It's not a trance. Now, you might have a good feeling, and there's nothing wrong with that, so long as you don't try to build a fence around it. The same goes for when you are having a hard time. Don't try to push it away, just be right there with it and see what happens. In Shambhala we call this unconditional allegiance to genuine life experience "warriorship" because it is a very brave way to live, on or off the meditation cushion. We can afford to experience life without filters.

Buddha nature is more like crystal clarity than a bed of pillows. It's delightful, but non-dwelling. You're just right here. It's not a trance.

Q. *My personal struggle is that I lost my mother only six weeks ago, and I am struggling with allowing her to move into the next life. Letting that attachment go is very real to me.*
A. Well, I think you should be kind to yourself. I don't think you should make too much of a project out of letting it go. Just experience it. Heartbreak has its own time. It's very beautiful.

Q. *We have a culture that doesn't acknowledge grief. Yeah, that makes sense. But that's my struggle; when I meditate I feel like I'm drowning in grief.*
A. Yeah, that's tough. Hang in there. Come and do group sitting. That's the thing to do. Cry in front of everybody. *(Laughter)*

Q. *Great!? (More laughter) Crying is good. I would say crying is very healing, isn't it. I always feel better after crying.*
A. Well you are kind of letting it all go. It's kind of a letting-go exercise. We are very present when we cry.

Q. *I never thought of self-pity as a form of aggression.*
A. It is the seemingly innocent rationale for perpetuating the endless cycle of aggression, which never stops until somebody deliberately eats it—that's warriorship. Ultimately everything is aggression if it is coming from the perspective of "me-ness".

The Third Noble Truth of Wealth

This talk was preceded by the discussion of the context of the shamatha meditation technique in Appendix B.

In this series of talks we have been discussing fundamental Buddhist teachings and making sure to include examples from economic life. By doing so, we are also exploring a more experiential understanding of wealth, and how that relates to economic life.

The first talk in the series was on inherent wealth and the idea that the way we usually pursue wealth has been frustrating. It has not brought us the satisfaction we thought it would, whether we attain financial success or not.

We raised the question whether the way we are defining wealth is the center of the problem, because if you define wealth in a relative sense it actually becomes a moving target. So we talked about the notion of inherent wealth, because what we ultimately want is that wealthy state of mind—and that is what we are expecting to get from our money in the end.

If our ultimate goal is a wealthy state of mind then we are actually pursuing wealth indirectly by pursuing it externally. The expectation is that we can use those resources to create a sense of wealthiness. Maybe we have notions of what creates a sense of wealthiness and we want to put in place all of those things. We may not think beyond that very often, but really what we are after is that sensibility, that very spacious, big state of mind that we associate with wealthiness. That fits very well into the spiritual journey, because it's a spiritual result that we are after. We have been struggling to work with the external world in hopes to bring about something that is decidedly internal.

*We are actually pursuing wealth
indirectly by pursuing it externally.*

Who knows what the macroeconomic implications of approaching wealth with such immediacy are? But it's probably a good idea to understand that sense of wealthiness better and establish it more effectively in the long-run and the short-run.

If the view that wealth is personally determined resonates with us, then we need to establish the ground of that view. The foundation of the Buddhist view of wealth and life altogether is encapsulated in The Four Noble Truths. It's one of the first teachings that the Buddha gave after attaining enlightenment.

The First Noble Truth is that life is suffering. The way we can wrap our heads around that is by contemplating impermanence. We have a lot of uncertainty in our lives that we try to ignore, deny, or sensationalize. But no matter what we do, all the things that are very dear to us, that we cherish, do get pried away from us sooner or later, or we get pried away from them. Then there are things that we don't want to come into our lives, that we try to ward off, and those things, of course, frequently do come in.

That is one of the foundations of the whole external wealth

struggle. We have a tendency to think of wealth as a kind of insurance policy to protect us against our fear—the ultimate fear being the fear of death. Death threatens to be everything that we don't want and take us away from everything that we do. Regrettably, everybody dies, without exception.

In The First Noble Truth talk, we examined suffering in greater detail. Buddhism invites us to not only accept our fear and pain but examine them objectively; to look closer and unpack the things that we normally avoid.

The Second Noble Truth is the truth of The Cause of Suffering. In this case we could call it The Second Noble Truth of wealth, the cause of the money/wealth struggle. Ultimately the cause of suffering from this point of view is clinging to the idea of a solid self, personality, or ego, which is a setup for stagnation and frustration.

If we examine the notion of ego, we find it is built out of assumptions. Some of those assumptions are questionable. Principal among these is that personal identity is static like a mountain. The systematic observation of meditation reveals that personal identity is more like a river, which looks the same but is completely fluid and changing from one moment to the next. The expectation that we could or should be solid sets up a mistaken frame of reference that seems constantly under attack. So in the Buddhist context, knowing "who you are" means knowing that mind is more like a whole theater company than one character in a play.

We call the struggle to support our solid and separate identities: ego clinging. Ego clinging is like a sly politician whose only real cause is to be in office. It puts a framework of logic around all of your experiences based on a separate you rather than appreciating each situation on it's own merits. It is very easy to progress from the belief in a solid ego to measuring every experience based on whether it supports you, threatens you, or doesn't matter to you or your chosen form of dogma.

Viewing the world from an egotistical point of view is like limiting your perception to a peephole in a fortress gate. You have made this huge assumption, which you don't realize is so huge. It seems very innocent, but you have made this assumption that you are separate, continuous, and defensible or supposed to be. The belief that me and mine are a separate entity legitimizes all of the things I might do to support that separate entity. This assumption makes the world a scary place; it walls us in. It also reduces altruism to just a stepping stone or distraction from one's main purpose, which is the perpetuation of "me".

Ego clinging is like a sly politician whose only real cause is to be in office.

The defensive poverty mentality of ego manifests in business as obsession with competition and marketing myopia. Fixating on covering our own needs removes us from the true needs and aspirations of others. The more preoccupied you are with yourself, the less open you become to the feedback of the marketplace and the needs of your customers. Your focus becomes very shortsighted.

Dwelling too much on ourselves we end up with a hit and miss experience over and over again. We might find economic life frustrating, but it's always frustrating from the point of view of a person or an objective. Your perception of the marketplace or your family, for that matter, becomes limited depending upon the degree to which it supports your latest egocentric agenda. An egotistical perspective is naturally insecure and constantly seeks reassurance from "the outside", if possible. But it turns out that the outside world is more like a river than a mountain too.

*Dwelling too much on ourselves we end up with
a hit and miss experience over and over again.*

One might think, "I shouldn't have to do the dishes again tonight. It's not my turn, it's not fair to me." And there's this competitive version of respecting our "selves" that clouds the direct perception of what needs to happen. It's earthy to have a chore chart and a well-thought-out business plan but we can also afford a little selfless service beyond the limits of egocentric logic to add real value, to a household, a company, or an economy. In fact it is the source of great joy in itself.

Buddhism invites us to examine all of our experience, including fear, which is a factor underlying much of our decision-making. The inseparable flipside of fear is hope - to get away from what we fear, far away. What drives fear? Maybe it is fear of pain, which we regard as a microcosm of death. Acknowledging and getting to know our fear has profound implications. In *Shambhala: The Sacred Path of the Warrior*, Chögyam Trungpa says 'curiosity about fear is the beginning of genuine fearlessness.'

*Chögyam Trungpa says 'curiosity about
fear is the beginning of genuine fearlessness.'*

Examining the nature of fear and suffering helps us to understand how we are self-perpetuating our own "cyclical existence" AKA struggle. Cyclical existence means that even though, every dog has his day, if you are out of touch, operating from an egotistical perspective, you will not manage your karmic return on investment very well and it is only a matter of time until you go back down again to the lower realms of experience. Your misplaced hope, fear, greed, guilt, or ignorance will handle all the travel arrangements for you.

You might become a really good bread salesperson, and convince a lot of people that eating white bread is great. You put all your creativity into packaging and selling it, because that's the bread with the biggest profit margin.

But have you really been open to other possibilities, like healthier kinds of bread? Maybe some are more labor intensive, so you would have to hire more people, endure more risk, or make it yourself. You can't make as much money from that; therefore, you don't even consider the possibility. So it follows that you can only consider making bread by machine. But then you find out some people are getting ill from products like yours. If your first priority is to make healthy food vs. profit, you can use this information to go in a completely different way.

If you are habituated to viewing the world defensively you might resist real change until the necessity of it clobbers you. At that point you might suddenly "get religion", quit your job, close the factory, throw everybody out of work, and miss a chance to migrate your industry in a better direction. Either way, it is the self-obsession that keeps us out of synch and going round in circles.

If we look at the egocentric approach in greater detail, we can see a lot more about what kind of life and society it puts together. Egotistical fixations crowd out fresh ideas that might be better for others, and for oneself in the long run. If you put yourself in the customer's shoes, you'll never be too far off track. What may be most valuable is selling their kids on healthy forms of bread. If maximum benefit to others is the key priority, then **service is the objective, profit is a constraint.** Management goal setting and creativity needs to be focused on creating policies and marketing mechanisms in line with that. A network of excellent bakers, for example, rather than a machine that transforms whole grains into bread that's only one step removed from sugar. Sorry, I don't mean to pick on the baking industry, it's just what came to mind.

Egotistical fixations crowd out fresh
ideas that might be better for others,
and for oneself in the long run.

Paradoxically, the first step to refocusing from egocentric to service oriented modus operandi is to make unconditional friends with oneself. It is the notions of personal inadequacy and related false urgency that rationalize simplistic, aggressive choices.

Our psychological identities are like a web of strings, the first strand being the assumption, "all this thinking must mean I exist! I think, therefore I am," which, without closer examination, quickly morphs into, "but I need to define myself better" and "now that I have decided I'm a man, a woman, a doctor, a lawyer, a meditator, an excellent mother, a noble servant of the shareholders, a consummate professional...I should be a certain way." In this way our relationship with the world, including with ourselves becomes conceptual and removed.

But the world is not actually party to our latest formula. So it's kind of like a calm ocean. On the days you imagine "ideal you", you're sailing along and the ocean is so calm. You've trimmed your sails for the breeze du jour and the sun is out. You are feeling like the world is validating you somehow. The next thing you know you are facing a headwind, and it feels like the world has turned against you. But really what's happening in our lives all the time is that the world is operating quite independently from our egocentric frame of reference. What we do is re-posture our egos constantly, searching for a magic formula that props up our assumption that we are one solid thing and we should be able to get it right and build ourselves up better—this time.

There is no end to strategies to prop up ego, increasing external wealth being one of the foremost. But the world is constantly poking in there. The world is like a cold breeze that blows up through our little tangle of string. Then it's suddenly cold inside our cocoon. So we spin a patchwork of logic to close off that draft of fresh air coming in, instead of appreciating the invigoration and clarity that it brings.

Recognizing the habitual process of ego, making itself up, strand by strand as we go along, frees us to relate with the world more honestly, accurately, and cheerfully. So the course correction becomes more like an ongoing dance than an endless quest for a permanent fix that causes a lot of additional pain or suffering. The real permanent fix is the deep understanding that there is no permanent fix possible or required.

The real permanent fix is the deep understanding that there is no permanent fix possible or required.

The Third Noble Truth (of Wealth)

Tonight we are going to talk about The Third Noble Truth, which is the truth of cessation. That it is possible to go beyond suffering or cease wallowing in it.

The good news about the cessation of suffering is that it is innate and ever-present. Inherent wealth is inherent. Underlying our human struggle is a basic human quality that is primordially pure. That sounds kind of fantastical, but there's no need for blind faith. We can actually get some experience of it and connect with it ourselves.

The cessation of suffering is what Prince Siddhartha discovered when he realized his original human nature was free of ego and naturally awake through sitting meditation. At that point he became known as Buddha, which simply means, "awakened one". He discovered that the foundation of who we are is already enlightened. In the Shambhala tradition we call this basic human nature "basic goodness", which doesn't mean morally good as opposed to bad, just that the fundamental foundation of human beings is unconditional pure and awake perception. We are talking about pre-ego reference points here. This "Basic Goodness", or "inherent wealth" as I am referring to it, is reflected in our ability to touch and be touched by the world, to have genuine raw perception free from the veils of ego.

> *The good news about the cessation of suffering is that it is innate and ever-present. Inherent wealth is inherent.*

All the interruptions and inconveniences that confront us each day; as well as the many ordinary moments of focus e.g. chopping vegetables, crossing the street, business transactions, any situation that demands or commands presence of mind has the potential to reconnect us with that basic quality, like cracks in a dam holding back a river of gold. From the Buddhist point of view basic goodness is where we come from and basic goodness is what we dissolve back into moment-by-moment. So it is both the ground and the fruition of our existence and non-existence for that matter. The path is to develop some familiarity with it so that we don't just zoom past, habitually recreating egocentric reference points.

The way to develop familiarity and confidence in the inexhaustible inherent wealth of basic goodness is through the practice of sitting meditation. Sitting meditation provides a very simple situation that gives the mind incredible space. Mind can run around in all directions, you can experience every emotion, but you just continue to bring it back to pure awareness.

What you find from that experience over and over is that you can afford to let go, you can live without a defensive mental game plan. In fact, you only really live your life in the gaps of the game plan! If you lean into that a little further, you might come to the realization that space, what occurs in those seemingly vacuous, un-defined, non-conceptual gaps in the habitual thought process, is spontaneously intelligent and reliable. You can actually trust space, you can have the game plan of no game plan, and then you can let go of that too.

You can actually trust space, you can
have the game plan of no game plan,
and then you can let go of that too.

Here are some of the qualities of cessation, which is the same as connecting with basic goodness or inherent wealth. It is unconditional; it is not something that is created or something you can lose. You don't get it, you didn't start it, it doesn't end. You can't screw it up even if you have been dishonest, irresponsible, impulsive, or cruel. It's innate to being human. You might not see it much if you are very depressed or confused, but it is still there, waiting for you.

It is ever-present, so you can actually be with it. Sounds like God, I know. *(Laughter)* It has no beginning or end. You can experience it best when your storyline breaks down or takes a break. It is the basically good, extremely perceptive, brilliant, primordially pure nature of mind before or underneath the habitual illusion of ego. We connect with it fleetingly already, without knowing or respecting it. It's least obstructed when we are completely present, synchronizing body and mind. It shines through in those microseconds when we are free of egotistical concerns.

Q. *It's called space, right?*
A. Yes, it is often referred to as "space," but it is also called Buddha nature, basic goodness, or inherent wealth. So it's quite the opposite of being, "spaced out". I guess that would be "spaced in". Even that sounds too complicated. It is utterly un-complicated space. Our basic nature is empty, yet luminous at the same time. Trungpa Rinpoche used to say that space is pregnant with intelligence and humor.

Another way to express The Third Noble Truth is that despite all of the self-criticism and emotions we allow to distract us, human nature is crystal clear, awake and complete. Intelligence, insight, and humor occur spontaneously, long before the English prose we mentally coach ourselves with. Taking a break from our storylines, in other words, taking them less seriously, leaves the gate of pure perception open longer. This uncontrived space of raw direct perception is the birthplace of energy, compassion, and wisdom.

Intelligence, insight, and humor occur spontaneously, long before the English prose we mentally coach ourselves with.

The key thing to get from The Third Noble Truth is the reliability of Buddha nature/basic goodness/inherent wealth/space at the foundation of your own humanity. In fact, basic goodness is the most profound and fundamental thing that all human beings have in common. Chögyam Trungpa called it our birthright.

Sakyong Mipham says wider understanding of basic goodness is the golden key to uplifting one's own life, and the whole of human society along with it.

This brilliant, pure, non-dual nature is there for all of us, without exception. Through contemplative practice, you can kick the tires on it and gradually learn to rely upon wide-open space as an alternative to endless webs of logic. We only need open the window to access it. How can we open such a window? Through the middle path, which is essentially the non-judgmental combination of gentleness and precision. It is only through the combination of relaxation with discipline that the window opens on Buddha nature. That is what the Buddha discovered. His prescription for how to connect with inherent wealth was the practice of sitting meditation and The Eightfold Path, which we will talk about next time.

The Fourth Noble Truth of Wealth

Good evening everyone. Welcome. This talk is called "The Fourth Noble Truth." The Fourth Noble Truth is the last of The Four Noble Truths; and The Four Noble Truths are, of course, a foundation teaching—one of the first teachings that the Buddha ever gave. We are putting a little spin on it because we are calling it The Fourth Noble Truth *of Wealth*. That just means we are going to talk about it with lots of examples from economic life.

We started out talking about inherent wealth. Inherent wealth is an alternative to thinking about wealth in the way that we usually do, which is to assume that wealth is something we get from outside, something we must bring in, or magnetize even.

The whole idea of inherent wealth is that everything is already there, here, here and there. Meaning wealth is already present, within us and around us, so there is a sense of completeness in the nature of things as they are.

The acquisition approach to wealth presumes that we need legal ownership of "every book in the library" in order to be made wealthy by it. Where's the fun in that? It's possible, can be done, to some extent, everybody would like to have more money, but we really should examine the motivating factors behind that habitual assumption because it is never enough at the end of the day.

All of us have had windfalls at various points in life. My experience is that they provide a temporary rush but passing benefit. You hope to get more money next time, because you think maybe that was the problem. Maybe you just didn't have quite enough or maybe you just screwed it up.

Really what it comes down to is that we want to get external things and money because we ultimately want to create the feeling of wealth, the confidence and heroism that we associate with it.

How do we spend our money? We spend our money as efficiently as we can to give us that feeling of wealth. Maybe you spend your money on investments, or maybe you want security for yourself and others, or maybe you want excitement or some interesting mix of everything you could get with money, a basket of goods and services optimized for maximum utility within a certain time frame. But ultimately what everyone wants is to feel good, right? It would be nice if one could feel good for a long time. But feeling good for a long time is more a product of understanding than fortification, and money can only do so much along those lines.

How do we spend our money? We spend our money as efficiently as we can to give us that feeling of wealth.

Even if we follow a spiritual path, there is no simple solution. We don't just acquire some realization and float above it all from then on. Life is still hard. There are sobering practicalities; the kids have to get fed, every day.

Nevertheless, the view of inherent wealth is that wealth is actually ever-present. If you have that kind of outlook, it helps on those days when you feel like there is nothing you can do. Our state of mind, including the sense of wealthiness, is always up to us, which is really good news.

The Four Noble Truths is a teaching that summarizes the spiritual path and establishes the foundation of the spiritual journey.

The First Noble Truth is The Truth of Suffering, which acknowledges that life is painful and a losing battle due to its impermanent nature, and also that trying to deny this basic reality causes way more pain. This additional pain is sometimes distinguished as suffering.

The Second Noble Truth is that there is a cause of that extra frustration and suffering, which is that we are approaching life dualistically. We are approaching it from the point of view of an ego.

The moment you consider yourself to be separate, the moment you consider your life experience to be independent of your projections about your life experience, you are fooling yourself. The carrot in front of you is actually attached to your back. You can't reach it, and everywhere you turn, it seems just out of your grasp because you continue to define success in a relative way. If we put that in the context of wealth, we can say that seeking a state of wealthiness externally is suffering. It is inherently frustrating; we can never get enough money to assuage our hope and fear, without coming to terms with them internally.

> *The carrot in front of you is actually attached to your back.*

But then just because it's hard to get, doesn't mean that it's not the answer, right? In fact, the harder something is to accumulate, the more precious it must be, right? It is particularly confusing because sometimes a little more money *is* exactly what we need.

One reason money is hard to accumulate is that contentment, not money, is our ultimate goal. We are only interested in money as a means to an end. We already know it's empty on some level, which is why we quickly lose the drive for it, maybe even a little too soon in some cases, in favor of more qualitative forms of wealth. In the back of our minds, we think we are just working this job to buy time. Nevertheless, there will never be enough money or time until we can appreciate life in a larger context. We will keep thinking we could find contentment with "something else" which money or time could buy, but that doesn't quite work. Seeking wealthiness through money is like using a toy hammer—it is symbolic of what we need and it might get the nail started, but it breaks down quickly from there. And the more nails you try to hammer with it, the less effective it becomes.

One reason money is hard to accumulate is that contentment, not money, is our ultimate goal.

So we need to appreciate the role of money and the richness of material things within our life as it is and not as another prerequisite for contentment. Working with money and livelihood is part of the spiritual path too.

The Third Noble Truth is the truth of cessation. For our purposes, this means that there could be an end to the money/wealth struggle. There is an end to the struggle that we experience around wealth, but maybe not where we have been assuming it is.

In the first two noble truths, the Buddha suggested closer examination of fear, pain, and suffering, that we stop and look at how we are operating, and acknowledge that this is a frustrating situation. Ask yourself, "How have I been pursuing happiness and how does it really come together and break down? What is it I'm really hoping for? What is it I'm really afraid of and why?"

The cessation of suffering is what we discover when we examine our experience in a larger context, when we take the cause of suffering out of the picture as much as we can. If suffering occurs because of ego clinging, then if you take the "me-ness" out of the equation, it becomes possible to see more clearly. One's perception is not clouded by taking it all so personally. The absence of ego effectively makes room for insight and energy to naturally occur. Life − Ego = Enlightenment, more simply, Egotism = Suffering, which is essentially The Second Noble Truth.

*Life − Ego = Enlightenment,
more simply, Egotism = Suffering,
which is essentially The Second Noble Truth.*

The Third Noble Truth refers to cessation, which rests in the space we discover in the absence of ego. This primordial purity is always there. We need only open to it through the gentle precision of contemplative practice, starting with sitting meditation.

The Fourth Noble Truth (of Wealth)

Liberating oneself from the suffering of egotism AKA poverty mentality is a process of transcending a prejudicial frame of mind. The tendency to reduce full-bodied life experience to the spectrum of good/bad/or unimportant for me and mine is a very narrow way to live. The contemplative approach is to think in terms of awareness vs. ignorance, which allows for a more unconditional appreciation of each moment.

The Fourth Noble Truth is that there is a path to the cessation of suffering. Since we are talking in terms of wealth and economics, we could call it the path to the cessation of poverty mentality. Poverty mentality is the habitual assumption that we need external reward or confirmation to rationalize everything we feel and do. In other words that we need to use external benchmarks to gage our worthiness as human beings.

Poverty mentality is the habitual assumption
that we need external reward or confirmation
to rationalize everything we feel and do.

The path is the way to apply oneself to overcome poverty mentality. What do we need to do? How should we regard our experience? What attitudes will help us form a lasting connection with inherent wealth? Upgrading attitudes is the first step toward transcending prejudice altogether.

We all maintain conscious and subconscious narratives about who we are. We cling to what's working for us and try to avoid what intimidates us. Sometimes you meet people who want to reassure themselves by telling you about how good it all is. I have a friend like that. When he is in the money, he can't wait to tell you about his latest conquest ad nauseum. And you're happy for him, but it's like, "Okay, I get it." (*Laughter*) (*Audience member: "Oh, and business is always getting better."*) Well, that's right, but then he goes silent when things aren't going as planned. My friend becomes a little depressed and a little angry. I have another friend who does just the opposite; she can't tell you enough about how tough her job is, but when things go well, she falls silent about it. In both cases, one side of the story supports the habitual narrative, the other doesn't. I've seen both patterns so often in myself that I have come to regard it as a tidal process.

When we are in a business situation like a networking party, sometimes we try to "act successful" as if we are deficient the way we are. Instead of engaging people openly and honestly, we try to armor up our persona—because you are "supposed" to do that; but such posturing is more transparent, than we imagine. On the other hand, there are tremendous opportunities for humor in these situations if we can relax a little. We might think, "Just making friends is so inefficient. I can't afford to just do that." But making genuine connections is the only thing worth doing, first or last.

Making genuine connections is the only thing worth doing, first or last.

From the Buddhist point of view, it's a lot more efficient to be open and genuine. It's more wealth-giving, both internally and externally in the long run. No one is going to enthusiastically support someone they don't know and trust, are they? So my strategy is to just make friends in these situations. Show up and try to extend myself to people. You never know how things will work out. Deep listening is the only discipline that need apply.

But if you are seeking to be more comfortable at trade shows, you may have come to the wrong talk; because my experience with the spiritual journey is that it gets worse before it gets better. You just get worse and worse at small talk for a while. It feels like everybody must be thinking, "What's going on with that person? He can't quite hold it all together."

When you are in the process of transition from guarded to genuine, emerging from your cocoon, your heart is more exposed; your game face starts to break down. You feel like you are naked in public because you are deliberately boycotting the agenda of ego, being more honest and less strategic. But you haven't made friends with yourself quite so unconditionally yet, so you feel exposed, but at the same time, something genuine is starting to happen. You want to call everyone up after the party and apologize, seek their absolution for the sin of having been so open. Nevertheless, my experience has been that people actually appreciate genuineness. Vulnerability is a window of opportunity for others to communicate genuinely and permission to be more open themselves in the future.

The question is: "If not from the point of view of ego, how should we operate? I mean, business has to get done, after all." The traditional teaching on The Fourth Noble Truth is **The Eightfold Path**. We could call it The Eightfold Path of wealth if you like. It is a spiritual approach, but it applies in economic life completely.

The Eightfold Path has three goals maybe because in order to bring about the cessation of suffering, we have to develop in three ways. Note that it is the cessation of suffering, not the cessation of pain. Pain is not going anywhere. You could say that suffering is the 99% unnecessary misery that comes from the expectation that pain is somehow avoidable or that vulnerability is a failure of some kind. We can make a better relationship to all aspects of our lives by seeing things in a larger context. The Eightfold Path helps us do that.

The Eightfold Path has three goals maybe because in order to bring about the cessation of suffering, we have to develop in three ways.

The first goal of The Eightfold Path is **moral sensitivity and compassion** for all living beings, including oneself. This means having a much more inclusive and far sighted definition of success.

The second goal of The Eightfold Path is **meditation**, which means peace and focus. Sometimes this is presented as meditative concentration or absorption, but it is essentially training oneself to be genuinely open—to be both vulnerable and confident at once. That's a challenge because we are habituated to seek strength by closing. Like a bad salesman putting on a suit of psychological armor before approaching people, we try to pretend that we are listening but we have such a narrow agenda that we don't dare be genuinely open. Being open seems too risky.

Meditation teaches us that it is possible to be very open and intelligent at the same time but that takes courage because it means a selfless point of view. In the context of economic life it is genuine professionalism, which is inquisitive and oriented towards mutual education; in contrast to professional arrogance, which is one-sided and insecure. Meditative concentration is an expression of confidence of the highest order because continuous awareness requires continuous exposure. I heard a foreign diplomat explain the same principle once. The concept of gentle warriorship applies. There are many situations where we must bravely serve the client's needs above our own. Being at home with uncertainty is at the heart of it.

Meditation teaches us that it is possible to be very open and intelligent at the same time.

The third and ultimate objective of The Eightfold Path is **transcendent wisdom**. Moral sensitivity and compassion may lead us to explore. That exploration could be through the vehicle of meditation. We might be inspired to explore meditation out of compassion for others. We have some understanding that the way we have been seeking happiness isn't working. Something's not quite right about the way we've been trying to nail down our world to make our lives better. It causes a lot of suffering all around.

Once we get into meditation, we discover it is the means of opening to wisdom. Wisdom is said to arise from the space of awareness—like the awareness we practice in meditative contemplation. So maybe there are a series of stepping-stones, from moral sensitivity and compassion to meditation and back again. All of this creates the energetic conditions for wisdom to occur in the form of insight, like lightning in space.

We might be inspired to explore meditation out of compassion for others.

There's kindness, then there's contemplation—going deeper, expanding awareness. Kindness and compassion displace ego. If we reduce ego a bit, awareness can expand because we are more open. We are not trying so hard to overlay our personal version of things on the world. In a business context, the more available we are to hear our customers, the more insights we have into the subtleties of their predicaments. That's wisdom. You could come up with solutions that might actually be helpful on many levels. Wisdom is the intelligence that arises from the space of awareness without ego.

Wisdom is the intelligence that arises from the space of awareness without ego.

We can get to higher levels of helping people based on awareness. Our communication becomes more accurate. Reducing neurotic speed, leaves room to take in more complete information. When we have that kind of awareness, wisdom spontaneously arises, sometimes in the form of humor. The Buddhist view is that this type of humor and intelligence are very close, if not the same thing. You could say that meditation is training oneself to be open to wisdom when it arises. If a sense of humor arises in the middle of an argument, are you prepared to let it through and diffuse the aggression? If a ray of sunshine penetrates your depression are you willing to cheer up?

When I was thinking about The Fourth Noble Truth I realized it's really about meditation. Meditation practice extending into meditation in action, that's the path. I had thought I would just give a talk on meditation because it unifies all of the different objectives of The Eightfold Path. And I don't usually think in terms of The Eightfold Path because it's too many things to remember. (*Laughter*) On the other hand, when I went through the traditional way of presenting The Fourth Noble Truth, I was reminded that there is a wider context and application of meditation in everyday life that I have been taught by my various teachers along the way. They have been putting these things in there all along and I am just now clueing in! Nevertheless, my experience is that all the steps of The Eightfold Path dawn on you eventually and become second nature through the practice of meditation.

> *All the steps of The Eightfold Path dawn on you eventually and become second nature through the practice of meditation.*

Another way to understand The Eightfold Path is that it is the healthy context of meditation. It is the way to live one's life with nobility and discover wealth both internally and externally. Although we refer to it in steps, it is really more like aspects. You could be working with any one or more than one at any time.

The Noble Eightfold Path

Right Understanding

The first step on The Eightfold Path is Right Understanding. Right Understanding is free from the two extremes of eternalism and nihilism. This is the distinction of Buddhism, in a certain way. Buddhism is called "the middle path" because it is free of these two extreme views. That said, I think all great traditions must recognize the importance of Right Understanding otherwise they can't last. I think all human beings who aspire to join a bigger view with practical existence probably end up in a very similar place.

The first of the two extremes, eternalism, is essentially putting all your eggs in the basket of the next life. You pretend that right and wrong is static, already figured out, therefore you don't have to relate fully and openly with others on the spot. You are just going to put all your hope and fear into a "blue chip" portfolio of pre-described pious attitudes and activities and then, presumably, you will find yourself in heaven. Life is basically a game of accumulating this cold conceptual version of merit and guarding your inflexible, rule based, version of virtue.

The trap of eternalism exists in every spiritual tradition including the ones that Prince Siddhartha followed before he became Buddha. Followers focused on putting down the cravings of this life, minimizing the body, regarding it as an obstacle to higher perception. The game plan of someone caught in the extreme of eternalism is to get onto what one believes is the "ultimate" spiritual high ground through a never-ending series of disciplines: self denials, self chastisement, body purification rituals, or heightened emotional states—e.g. fasts, diets, personal training, strategic philanthropy, or maybe even a suicide mission. Another version of eternalism is going around chasing confirmation from the highest best gurus.

Another version of eternalism is going around chasing confirmation from the highest best gurus.

There are lots of us who go too far with all that. The essence of it is the obsession with being "good" to the point that it becomes divisive with others. It is spiritual materialism. From the Buddhist point of view, just being "good" won't liberate you, or anyone else, from suffering. It won't quite work because it's still about "me." You end up going back down to the lower realms because ego is still involved. The Buddhist perspective is that virtue without the spacious/playful view of egolessness brings only temporary benefits, at best.

Eternalism is being blind to how subjective or "pre-packaged" one's definition of "good" is. It can become so unbalanced and suffocating, you end up doing little—or big—nihilistic, "bad" things that get you into trouble, or just expanding your definition of good to rationalize what you want. TV preachers, politicians, and doping athletes come to mind, but another example of eternalism is overzealous parents who impose "good" habits heavy handedly, neglecting the cost to the child's self-esteem and maturation process. You can get lost in how things look vs. how they are on the deeper levels that count. Overzealous activists and ideologues get stuck in a version of eternalism too.

The second of the two extremes is **nihilism**. Nihilism is looking for satisfaction and protection entirely in the things and pleasures of this life. This includes trying to rationalize everything back to the material plane. The focus is consumption and accomplishment oriented: where the best bargains are, where to vacation, what kind of car to buy, which shows to watch, groups to join, and the best way to become a general—never mind which army. You wake up in the morning busy with thoughts of how you are going to entertain or advance yourself today. Nihilism in the extreme is that selfish mindset, which doesn't consider any larger moral/ethical context beyond one's own advantage. You burn through your life with no inspiration greater than the possessions or status you can pile up. Sometimes the extreme of nihilism takes the form of religiosity where people join and switch congregations based on prospective networking benefits.

When I was an investment advisor, there were colleagues who appeared to make all their mutual fund recommendations based upon the qualifications for the next sales reward trip. Maybe they figured there was uncertainty in every recommendation, so they just gave up trying and served themselves.

In a larger context, nihilism is giving up consideration for how your business or activity contributes to the world—ignoring the implications of using your energy in ways that may be at cross purposes with the larger social/environmental benefit. For example, fast food companies seeking higher profit margins by normalizing oversized soft drinks or financial institutions promoting high interest credit cards as "financially responsible" because their focus groups indicate that's how people desperately want to feel. The numbers are driving the product development bus too much.

Nihilism is giving up consideration for how your business or activity contributes to the world

---

Both of those are examples of giving up. It is a backwards approach and very cynical. Why not sponsor nutritional research and be the first to offer solutions for people to eat healthier? Or set up installment plans to help customers save up for major purchases in advance because you yourself know how much better that feels?

Free market economists might argue, "oh, the invisible hand will take care of it." Maybe so, but the consumer decisions that guide the invisible hand are driven by aspiration and intention. Just because you can make a buck on impulse buying, doesn't mean people wouldn't much prefer help to bridge the gap between their highest intentions and immediate needs. Everyone wants to be able to afford a globally sustainable and socially beneficial balanced life. There is an egoless hero inside each one of us that wants nothing more than to participate in the creation of enlightened society. Why not make your business facilitate that?

There is an egoless hero inside each one of us that wants nothing more than to participate in the creation of enlightened society.

Both customers and investors are beginning to track this kind of "Karmic ROI". The world has to make some hard right turns socially and environmentally now, so why not incorporate that into the business model proactively? Chögyam Trungpa said that enlightened society is realized not in spite of private enterprise but through it. It has to be that way because economic activity is so all encompassing. Luckily customers and investors are eager for inspiration beyond green packaging.

On a more personal level, buying a brand new gas-guzzler or ignoring the municipal recycling program could be examples of nihilistic behavior. You are cynical that what you do makes any meaningful harm or benefit, so you over-prioritize your own comfort and privacy rather than looking for more inclusive solutions. That's nihilism.

Nihilism and eternalism are both ways we lose communication with our world. What you lose in both cases is the well being of loving kindness toward oneself and the bliss of community with others.

Nihilism and eternalism are both ways we lose communication with our world.

Buddhist art often depicts fierce deities with symbolic jewelry and gestures. One of the aspects you often see is an enlightened deity with one foot stepping on a naked woman and the other foot stepping on a pious monk holding ritual objects. Those two represent nihilism and eternalism respectively. The message is that Right Understanding is not nihilism and not eternalism. Nevertheless, when asked why the deity in one image had one leg straight and the other slightly bent, Chagdud Tulku Rinpoche explained, 'it's probably best to lean a little more toward the next life!'

So freedom from the two extremes is Right Understanding. What it boils down to is that we must use our hearts as well as our minds to determine the best way forward for all concerned, in every situation.

Right Thought

The second step on The Eightfold Path is Right Thought. And again, these two, Right Understanding and Right Thought are connected with wisdom. It is important to note that thoughts, emotions, and actions are often progressively linked, but they are also just expressions of energy. As such we don't have to take the content so seriously and can make a fresh start at any moment.

I think much of The Eightfold Path is meant to illuminate the karmic chain of events. The point of Right Thought is not so much that you can control your thoughts, but to understand that whatever trains of thought you indulge have a tendency to grow. Whatever you're dwelling on will link up to emotion and actions sooner or later and impact the lives of others.

Right Thought is acknowledging the power of thought content, and recognizing your habitual thought patterns. It is the practice of training oneself back from negative thoughts and applying a cheerful state of mind. Cheerful means not losing one's sense of humor vs. insisting that things are going to get "better". The recognition of pain and habitual mental storylines can even be reminders to come back to the present. The instruction is not to push thoughts away, which would be counter-productive anyway, but just to witness them and let them dissolve by themselves.

Cheerful means not losing one's sense of humor
vs. insisting that things are going to get "better".

Until we start to examine things more closely, we assume our thoughts are independent, which they are at the first thought level perhaps; but after that they become quite habitual i.e. repetitive patterns that we can recognize and relax our investment in quite a bit. Widening our perspective through meditation practice helps us gain understanding of how thoughts turn into emotions and then actions. We can choose to avoid dwelling on any particular line of thinking too much. After all, insight and intelligence occur long before the words we use to mentally coach ourselves with.

Insight and intelligence occur long before the
words we use to mentally coach ourselves with.

The practice of Right Thought has a quality of gently reeling our emotions in or simply choosing more uplifted interpretations of experiences incorporating awareness of basic goodness. It has a light touch quality opposed to heavy-handed judging oneself. Right Thought is being awake and aware of what our own line of thinking is, and choosing to let things go. In other words, not being at the mercy of, or fortifying your position with whatever logic happens to be going on in your mind. It's like supervising children at play—we can discriminate between what kinds of play are likely to work out and what's likely to end badly. Put another way, we can afford to be reasonable people. Contribute our perspectives without making a self-righteous identity out of them.

For example, if your partner wakes you up in the middle of the night or your supervisor corrects you on something at work, you might find yourself spinning a whole story about how inconsiderate he or she is. You overlay a very negative persona on them to justify your own irritation. It's like putting on evil sunglasses that filter out their basically good nature. There's no problem with feeling whatever we feel, including irritation. The problem comes when we fail to let things go and try to justify the negativity with blame. The more familiar we are with habitual thought patterns, the sooner we can recognize and let go. They become reminders to wake up in themselves.

Right Thought is working with your life, beginning even at the thought level. So it is being aware of your own mental environment and choosing to uplift your head and shoulders, accommodate positivity and relax negativity. It should be understood to be a mindfulness practice of opening up vs. shutting down, and not another means of judging oneself.

Right Thought is working with your life, beginning even at the thought level.

Right Speech

The next three steps on The Eightfold Path are Right Speech, Right Action, and Right Livelihood. These are associated with the development of compassion. They are pretty similar to Right Thought. Perhaps compassion is how wisdom manifests when it's out in the world.

Right Speech is being mindful of our speech and aware that how we speak sets up our world. When we speak in an angry tone, we end up living in solidified world, or a world where others do not trust us. We come off so hot headed they think we might sue them in court or judge them too harshly, which makes everyone defensive, they dig into their positions or withhold valuable input.

Right Speech is being mindful of our speech and aware that how we speak sets up our world.

Sloppy speech has unexpected repercussions, like when you overhear your 11-year-old scolding your 7-year-old in the same cruel tone that you used on her. By the same token, kind words can go a long way toward creating a kind world by way of their gentleness as much as their content. Your words carry more weight and people listen more subtly if you engage them with confidence and gentleness. The discipline of Right Speech also applies to email and other forms of communication.

Chögyam Trungpa made a connection between good posture and Right Speech. In *Shambhala: The Sacred Path of the Warrior*, he said it's very rare to see someone with good head and shoulders barking out harsh words at others. Maybe we should sit up straight while writing and reviewing emails too.

Another aspect of Right Speech is listening. Genuine listening is a profound expression of generosity and an expression of egolessness on the spot. It hones our responses and helps others to trust and listen to us.

Finally, frivolous speech blocks out more genuine communication and the perception of the sacred world.

Right Action

Something that I neglected to say at the beginning of this section is that The Eightfold Path is actually called The Noble Eightfold Path. It is helpful to connect with that image of nobility, because this path is the heart essence of nobility. The Eightfold Path is a helpful reference point for the way to carry on in your life with wisdom, compassion, and elegance. It really spells it out for us. Right Action is considering the momentum created by aggressive actions or neglectful in-actions, and the positive repercussions that come from acts of kindness.

Right Action is considering the momentum created by aggressive actions or neglectful in-actions, and the positive repercussions that come from acts of kindness.

Right Livelihood

The instruction on Right Livelihood is simply to seek livelihood or ways of conducting one's livelihood that don't involve causing harm to others. It is even better to make a livelihood in ways that are especially helpful, but simply uplifting your existing industry / work situation may be the most profound approach. The inspiration that motivates us is the key ingredient. The compassionate intention and good cheer with which we conduct ourselves in whatever job we have will have ripple effects far beyond the workplace.

Presumably one could avoid becoming a loan shark, but there is no prescription for what work you should be doing. In the immediate sense, the work we should be doing is the work we are doing, even if it is the work of looking for work. The essence of Right Livelihood is in the good will and the way of relating with everyone that comes in to it: customers, clients, competitors, colleagues, etc. There are amazing possibilities in that. You could make a genuine connection with each person you deal with. There is a synapse that occurs each time you shake someone's hand, give change, answer the telephone, or choose words for an email. Being completely present and honest creates tremendous space for your own relationships and reverberates far into the world through the lives of the people you meet.

Being completely present and honest creates tremendous space for your own relationships and reverberates far into the world through the lives of the people you meet.

I think there are interesting possibilities to create prosperity just by infusing egoless awareness into the activities of daily economic life. It is possible to create a genuine connection with each person you deal with even if it is only for one second, without any words. It has been said that 90% of communication occurs beyond words anyway.

On the other hand, I have been getting a lot of cold calls lately. Some of them are from Asia, some of them are from distant parts of North America. It's interesting, the accents you get. Ironically, since they started the 'do not call' list, local business people are afraid to call you, but the number of distant cold calls at home and work has doubled. More than once I have put one on hold, only to discover a second one on the other line. When business is slow, sometimes cold-callers are the only people who call me. Good grief! But I have started to be kinder to them. It isn't easy, because they seem like such pests, and they are proactively trying to get a foot in. Nevertheless, even though one must decline most offers fairly quickly, I have started trying to be very present with them, as much as I can. So every phone call is a contemplative opportunity to watch mind closely and develop discipline, patience, and kindness.

Every phone call is a contemplative opportunity to watch mind closely and develop discipline, patience, and kindness.

Remember when you're on the phone with somebody, that you are talking with a human being (like you), and that person is having a day, pain of alternation, pain of pain, a day of life, just like you, and they probably don't make much money, face a lot of uncertainty, and you're probably going to tell them something they don't want to hear. It is possible to relate with them kindly or even playfully on some level, and that has reverberations for both of you. He or she is going to be on the phone with somebody else in a second, and so might you, or someone might walk into your office. We should be aware that whatever energy we bring forth, anger or compassion, affects us long after the event. Right

Livelihood is bringing awareness to all our activity at work and home like that.

A last perspective on Right Livelihood is relating earnestly to whatever livelihood you have. The opportunity in this life, or any life is not as much in what we do as in how we do it. It's very easy to rationalize a less-than-wholehearted dispatch of our duties in a job that we consider beneath us or distasteful, or above us for that matter. But if we look at it from a karmic perspective, there are a million reasons why we have ended-up in the particular spot we are in, including our dead-end jobs. And there is no escaping the fact that each moment of our lives is always the next step on our path. You could say the only thing we really have to work with is attitude. Eventually, attitude affects everything else.

The opportunity in this life, or any life is not as much in what we do as in how we do it.

Whatever job we happen to be in at the moment, the best way forward usually includes cheering up and doing the best that we can. It's possible to do that while still acknowledging whatever we feel and trusting our own assessment of the environment.

Chögyam Trungpa said working through karma is "like wearing out an old pair of shoes." From that cosmic, karmic, point of view no earnest effort is wasted. So we could embrace whatever job we are in wholeheartedly as a spiritual challenge/path. We could try to improve the situation for the benefit of those we interact with and for those who will replace us. Sometimes that means giving honest feedback to an overbearing boss or a mindless bureaucracy, even when we fear the repercussions. It's not just about us; it is about uplifting the whole situation, including the well-being of your boss.

*From that cosmic, karmic, point of
view no earnest effort is wasted.*

Giving feedback is a two way street, of course. There can be a lot of fear associated with honest communication, which is why it is important to remain open and gentle, apply the discipline of Right Speech. On the receiving end, it is a great gift to be able to pluck the pearls of insight even when they are packaged in a mountain of hyper-critical manure.

*On the receiving end, it is a great gift
to be able to pluck the pearls of insight
even when they are packaged in a
mountain of hyper-critical manure.*

Right Effort

The last three steps—Right Effort, Right Mindfulness, and Right Concentration—are associated with the development of meditative awareness. Why is meditation presented last? Maybe it's because meditation facilitates the whole path.

Right Effort usually refers to our effort in meditation practice, but we work with it moment by moment as well. There are two types of effort that go into meditation practice. The first is the effort to get yourself onto the cushion. Get thee to the meditation hall! So you showed Right Effort today when you came to this talk. You overcame the fatigue tempting you for the nihilistic comfort of your TV. That is very good. We have to put ourselves out like that. There are lots of times when we know that if we apply ourselves it is going to be wholesome. Showing up will create a circle of virtue. Ironically, going to bed on time is like that too. You have to cut off the search for entertainment, or confirmation even in the form of work.

Healthy situations are sometimes hard to get to. You might feel a little better because you just thought of doing something virtuous. When it's time to actually make the intimidating out-going sales calls or go meditate, you think, "I already feel much lighter, so I don't need to go." Unfortunately, the good feeling fades quickly when you don't follow through with the wholesome activity. Nevertheless, Right Effort is also resisting the coun-terproductive urge to motivate yourself through self-criticism when you resist or fail. Self-deprecation is missing the point in much the same way as self-aggrandizement; both are denials of inherent wealth.

Self-deprecation is missing the point in much the same way as self-aggrandizement; both are denials of inherent wealth.

The second, more subtle and profound version of Right Effort occurs within one's mind. You apply it in your meditation practice. Making the effort to apply the meditation technique earnestly is very powerful and beneficial, because the training carries over when you are off the cushion. And in the same way, not applying Right Effort, not making the effort to return to being present, especially in the context of meditation practice, is counter-productive.

"Laziness" in the context of awareness practice means not mak-ing the effort to slow down and apply the meditation technique.

You just end up spinning your wheels. Meditation can be hard work. Right Effort also means being willing to begin at the beginning. Genuine intention is the key.

The practice of Right Effort could also be applied to work/life balance. Just like the reasoning mind can never acquire enough money to reassure it, that same mentality can prevail at work. Once we accomplish one thing, it's natural to want to accomplish more. Without the discipline of Right Effort telling us to pack it in, pretty soon we are seeking results in a greedy way that competes with the reason we took the job in the first place, presumably to create a healthier world for everyone, including our families. Life without balanced effort becomes an unsustainable vicious cycle.

Creating a balanced life requires accepting a greater degree of uncertainty AKA bravery. After all you could reassure yourself by constantly putting more time in at work. But managing your time to keep things in proportion is actually more efficient in the end. Being a workaholic is a great example of poverty mentality, because it drags down creativity and perpetuates a sense of struggle.

So Right Effort is applying discipline gently and extending oneself in healthy ways. That also means keeping some balance by renunciating certain indulgences, even if they are in a form that is socially condoned. It's like making the effort to eat healthy food first, which, in the meditation context, means applying oneself to the technique. The ROI of better focus and time management is higher than extended hours anyhow.

Right Mindfulness

Right Mindfulness is similar to Right Effort. Again, we are talking about meditative awareness here. Right Mindfulness has to do with being aware of the energy of mind vs. the content, which is more in the realm of Right Thought. So Right Mindfulness is attentive in a non-judgmental way like headlights are attentive to objects on a highway or like sun is attentive to fog. It could also be described as awareness of how we feel vs. what we think.

Right Mindfulness has to do with being aware of the energy of mind vs. the content, which is more in the realm of Right Thought.

Along the lines of Right Mindfulness, my teacher made a clear distinction between cynicism and healthy skepticism. At one time he proposed establishing community groups called deleks. The word *delek* means fortress of joy. Under the delek system, meditation practitioners in a neighborhood and friends, often from very different backgrounds, organize potlucks and generally get to know each other. It is a local, organic, slow moving social network and a spiritual practice of extending oneself all in one!

Nevertheless, some of Chögyam Trungpa's students were immediately cynical about this new initiative when he first brought it up. We felt over-extended already and didn't want to be bothered with extending ourselves to strangers, so we were critical before even trying it, and not in a constructive way. He took advantage of the situation to point out; that particular type of negativity needs to be pruned. People who wish to do something genuine, something good, should not be automatically criticized or made fun of, but should be constructively encouraged.

This is a subtle but important point. One of the wonderful things about Shambhala and Buddhism in general is that healthy skepticism, or critical intelligence is encouraged; but here he distinguished that from cynicism. Cynicism is a form of laziness, or debilitating doubt, that leads to depression. It is a habitual tendency to be critical.

Right Mindfulness is being aware of our own subtle motivation.

We should make the distinction between skepticism and cynicism internally as well. If we want to try something, especially if it is altruistic, we should consider it carefully but dare to experiment. We should not be afraid to try, even if we feel a little exposed. We can afford to take such leaps so long as we can remain genuinely open to the feedback. That is the distinction between expressions of confidence vs. aggression. Aggression is pre-emptory and defensive.

Right Mindfulness is being aware of our own subtle motivation.

For example, I wanted to give these Inherent Wealth talks because I wanted to do the research and discuss these ideas. I didn't know if anybody would be interested. *(laughter)* If I felt people would criticize me a lot for trying, I might have hesitated to do it, and I think that would have been too bad.

You can see how understanding the distinction between skepticism and cynicism is key in the organizational context. Many groups choke off their own creativity unwittingly by not recognizing the distinction. If people become fearful of experimenting or exposing their inspiration, energy will dissipate, innovation will cease. Many romantic couples undercut themselves by over-indulging cynical styles of humor.

So Right Mindfulness is being alert not only to the content of our thoughts but also to the quality of the energy behind them, such as the urge to prejudge situations at the earliest stage, just because you can.

Right Concentration

The last but not least aspect of The Noble Eightfold Path is Right Concentration. Right Concentration has to do with putting out that last 20% of effort. It is maintaining openness and applying the effort to really enter into contemplative space, contemplative mind, again and again. Right Concentration is believing in yourself—whether you are on or off the meditation cushion. It is not indulging feelings like, "I couldn't possibly do that!" Enlightenment is actually on the table. You could actually drop everything and be fully awake on the spot, right now. It is only our habitual assumption of ego that holds us back and that's flickering already. You could actually embody primordial purity, right now.

Enlightenment is actually on the table.
You could actually drop everything and
be fully awake on the spot, right now.

In economic life, Right Concentration manifests as strong determination to accomplish what you wish to accomplish. It is said that strong determination is a source of joy because if you have strong determination to do something, it is only a matter of time until you accomplish it.

So Right Concentration is not to assume otherwise. Don't assume that, because you are just a novice, it's not that important to focus. You can actually be a *mahasiddha* (enlightened being) on the spot. (*Audience member: "I should be so lucky!"*) Well, don't be cynical, that's Right Concentration!

Conclusion to The Eightfold Path

The Four Noble Truths and The Noble Eightfold Path are the way that we progress from acting clever to being wise—in other words, how we can make our lives more cheerful in a lasting way. That is the subtlety of the different aspects we discussed, like avoiding the two extremes.

How do you become stronger but remain vulnerable and open to feedback? Those two need to be combined because otherwise it is just cyclical existence. If you have one without the other you will just take the bait of ego and go back around the miserable cycle of passion, aggression, and ignorance again and again.

Q. *That is very difficult, to be open and confident at the same time—the devil is in the details. At different times it seems that different levels of openness are called for.*
A. What do you mean, different levels of openness?

Q. *In terms of a professional relationship, there are times when I need to reflect; there are times when it is helpful to share my own experience, and there are times when it is not. There are some people who have pathologies where they pull energy from other people and at those times you need to be less open, because it is not actually helpful to them or to you to have that energy pulled out of you.*
A. I see, yes, I think openness is more in terms of attitude rather than the duty of spelling everything out all the time. Your intuition, meaning insight without ego, also known as discriminating awareness wisdom or prajna, helps you decide how to be in each situation. It is not just attempting to force a simplistic idea of openness. That would be naïve. On the other hand, discriminating awareness wisdom arises from space. So we have to be unscripted, and very on the spot to access it.

I know what you mean though. It's challenging to communicate in a genuine yet skillful way.

Being genuine has the quality of curiosity. You are mindful of the messages that the situation is giving you, which makes you better prepared to make a decision. There is no game to win in an egotistical sense. You are not trying to manipulate or guard your own ego but rather you are just putting the round pegs in the round holes according to the natural flow of the situation. This impartial view makes one hard to predict or manipulate.

Being genuine has the quality of curiosity.

Continuity of awareness provides the means to make good decisions. There is a Buddhist slogan, "Of the two, hold the principle witness." Which means listen to everyone but trust your own best take of what's going on, internally and externally. Go with your intuition of what makes most sense for all concerned and see what happens. You may be right or you may be wrong but it is the way to learn.

Conclusion

The Four Noble Truths of Wealth is a foundational view statement for the spiritual path of economic life. The spiritual journey is a process of developing the ability to discriminate between genuine prosperity, which is based on clarity, and the shortsighted approach of materialism, which is based on objectifying oneself and others.

If we want to find lasting prosperity we have to first understand that wealth is always a matter of perception. Recognizing this informs our actions and enables us to discover the genuine confidence of wealthiness more directly.

Fixating on external wealth exclusively is a set up for frustration because not only are the objects that mind desires constantly breaking down or changing value, but mind itself is constantly changing too. So pursuing wealth without understanding the significance of one's own mind to the ultimate sense of prosperity is like filling a bucket with a hole in the bottom.

From the Buddhist point of view, the wealth of human beings is inherent in our capacity to perceive and appreciate our world and our experience, whatever it may be. Thus it is ever present. The experience of wealthiness has more to do with a wealthy outlook, than any particular set of circumstances.

Meditation makes us wealthier by opening up a direct appreciation of our experience as it is. The more aspects of our experience we appreciate, the more genuinely confident and the less panicked we are.

So an enlightened approach to economic life is based on awareness and activity that opens connections to inherent wealth in oneself, others, and the world around us. The Noble Eightfold Path is a description of how to stay connected with the inexhaustible treasure of inherent wealth in the course of daily life.

A connection to inherent wealth occurs whenever we synchronize our body and mind. Whenever we are fully present and free of egotistical pre-occupation, the window of inherent wealth is open.

A deeper understanding of wealth comes in through direct, non-judgmental perception and reverberates through our actions as depicted by The Noble Eightfold Path. It organically engenders well-being in others, which creates enlightened economy and enlightened society on the spot.

Appendix A: Meditation Instruction

This meditation instruction was given in the hour preceding the talk on The Second Noble Truth (of Wealth).

View

Welcome. It's traditional to begin Buddhist teachings or meetings with a bow. In this context a bow is just an expression of mutual respect and also to create a kind of sacred space, "sacred" meaning a space of awareness. So the idea is to create a wholesome situation for learning and communication.

According to the tradition of bowing that I have learned, you put your hands together at the heart level gently like this and then you bow, nodding from the top of your head. You wouldn't necessarily bow deeply in this instance. The depth of the bow has to do with the rank of the teacher, and also the significance or depth of the teaching situation. So if you were receiving a very high, advanced teaching, you might do a very deep bow at that point. But for our purposes we could just do a simple bow like this.

Q. *No prostration? No full body prostration?*
A. Well, maybe in your case.
   (Laughter)

Then there is the Shambhala bow, which is a more secular version. It's more like a samurai warrior bow—essentially it is the same, except you put your hands on your hips. Either way, don't forget to rest in pure awareness for a moment when you come back upright. That's the fruition of the whole thing.

Tonight I'm going to give a very brief instruction on shamatha meditation. Shamatha is a style of meditation that translates as "calm abiding" or "resting the mind." It is a very straightforward meditation technique that was taught by my teacher, Chögyam Trungpa Rinpoche. He recommended that shamatha be practiced regularly by beginners and experienced practitioners alike. Later it is also used to sandwich other forms of meditation. You will usually begin and end with shamatha. So it is an excellent entry-level practice and a complete fruition practice as well.

Before going into the details of the technique itself, I should say that the view of Buddhism is that we are fundamentally awake, fundamentally enlightened as human beings already. The purest gold is already present. The practice of meditation and the study of Buddhism is really a path of removing obstacles to our natural intelligence, which is 100% present, here and now. Our basic state of being is in harmony with the environment when we synchronize our body and mind.

The practice of meditation and the study of Buddhism is really a path of removing obstacles to our natural intelligence

---

Most of the time we go through life fogged-in by our own habitual commentary—constant mental chatter. We are self-coaching, categorizing and strategizing everything that's going on with surprisingly little direct perception. It is a constant distraction from simply being where we are. It is so ubiquitous that we hardly notice it's going on until we sit still.

What we are practicing in this form of meditation is simply being fully present in our bodies, right where we are, to feel what we feel and see what we will see on any level. We are just going to switch our allegiance to being here now.

The Practice

The basic shamatha meditation technique is to sit in an upright posture and breathe. Just be in your body. Feel what it is to be right here, breath going in and out, experience your sense perceptions including mental activity. When you find yourself distracted by daydreams, aches, pains, strong emotions, gently bring yourself back to just being in your body, breathing, awake, in the room, on the earth. That's it.

The basic shamatha meditation technique is to sit in an upright posture and breathe.

Sound easy enough? That is all you need to do. We give the introduction like that now because it's easy to become distracted with trying to perfect the details of the traditional instruction and miss the forest for the trees, so to speak. It's about being present. Just hold yourself upright and keep tuning-in to being where you are. It's almost as if your nervous system starts to extend to include everything in your field of perception. Every distraction or sensation is actually part of being present. Another metaphor is breathing through every pore in your body.

That is the heart of it. In case it helps, here is the traditional shamatha meditation instruction as as well.

The first part of shamatha meditation is the six points of posture.

1. SEAT. The first part of the posture is to take your seat and feel very much grounded on your bottom. Rooted, you could say, similar to yoga imagery. So you have a good foundation in the center of your seat.

2. LEGS. Then your legs are loosely crossed in front, or if you are in a chair, they can be straight down in front of you with your feet flat on the floor. It's ideal to sit on a meditation cushion in the traditional cross-legged posture described here, but you can sit in a chair or on a bench if a suitable cushion is not available or if the traditional posture is too difficult. No problem.

3. ARMS. Let your arms drop directly down from your shoulders and hang loosely. Then lift your hands, bending at the elbows, and set them down gently wherever they naturally land on your thighs.

4. TORSO. Your torso comes up like a tree trunk. Imagine you are like a tall tree that comes up naturally with a sense of natural dignity, "head and shoulders." Hold your head up straight as if there is a string gently pulling on the top of your head toward the sky. Your shoulders are relaxed and your heart is open. So you are exerting a little effort to hold yourself upright, but in a relaxed way.

   Imagine your vertebrae are stacked on top of each other, so you have the feeling of balancing a broomstick. The broomstick will pretty much hold itself up with very little effort if you just apply a little ongoing attention to keep it upright and not leaning off-center too much one way or the other.

5. EYES. Your gaze should be slightly downward and unfocused. Resist the urge to look for patterns on the floor. Just let your eyes rest there and keep it simple. So you maintain awareness

of the whole room, but your gaze is downward at the angle of about six feet in front of you, and unfocused.

6. MOUTH. Finally, relax your jaw. Let your mouth be open just a tiny bit, almost imperceptibly, and rest your tongue behind your top front teeth. Breathe naturally through your nose and a tiny bit through your mouth as well.

There is an overall sense of being present, open, and dignified just as you are.

You could begin by trying that posture for a few minutes. Chances are you will find some part of your posture will drift out of alignment. For a lot of us the head tends to come forward. Whenever you recognize this, resist the urge to criticize yourself. Just gently correct your posture. The work of maintaining a sense of body that is upright yet relaxed is actually part of the practice discipline. On the other hand, if you feel overwhelmed you can drop the whole technique and make a fresh start at any time. Good head and shoulders alone is very powerful, whether you are on or off the meditation cushion.

Good head and shoulders alone is very powerful, whether you are on or off the meditation cushion.

Tune-in to how it feels to just be here, in your body, in the room. Aches, pains, sounds, distractions of any kind are all part of the landscape. Just notice them but try to resist dwelling on anything. Come back to feeling your breathing and your body, without any judgment as much as you can.

(Sit for 5 minutes.)

Beyond maintaining a relaxed and upright posture, the only physical reference point is to be aware of your breath coming and going naturally. We place our mindfulness on the reference points of the body and the breath because they are the simplest and closest to just being present, which is our aim.

The next part of the shamatha meditation technique is working with the thoughts that arise. The instruction for relating with thoughts is not to judge them, or yourself, as good or bad. The practice has a quality of "touch and go." Try to notice you are thinking without getting caught-up in the storyline of any given thought. If you like, you can say to yourself the word "thinking" to help you let go and then just go back to awareness of the breath. Imagine your thoughts passing out into the room and dissolving into the air along with each out-breath. You can even imagine that you yourself are dissolving with your breath into the pure awareness of the room. Either way, you are just being here, wide-awake and completely present.

The instruction for relating with thoughts is not to judge them, or yourself, as good or bad.

Finally, resist the urge to make a big project out of perfecting or customizing the meditation technique in any way. We are just making a relationship with raw experience. Try to apply yourself to it as described, as earnestly as you can. Experienced meditators catch themselves continuously, straightening their posture as needed, noticing their daydreams and coming back to the basics very naturally without being self-critical. You just do your best to keep your attention coming back to being in your body, in the room, completely awake, simple as that.

It's important to understand that in shamatha meditation we are not trying to create any particular state of mind, our only objective is pure, uncontrived perception. The reference points of the posture and the breath are only meant to give us the simplest touchstone possible so we can be free to witness the landscape of each moment, including mind going through its habitual gyrations. (Sit for 10 minutes.)

You just do your best to keep your attention coming back to being in your body, in the room, completely awake, simple as that.

The Gong

When you come to a typical meditation session, you come in and sit down, get comfortable on your seat and take your posture, upright yet relaxed. You settle yourself into the technique, eyes slightly downward, unfocused, aware of your breath, and dissolving into pure awareness with each out-breath as described above. Then the timekeeper (a.k.a. Umdze), which might be yourself, will ring the gong.

If you can get yourself established before the gong rings, you can use the ring down of the gong to seal you into your practice. Try to hold completely still for as long as you can. This will help you get off to a good start. There is really no such thing as a bad start or bad meditation practice mind you. Just do your best to be present and aware of your mind. You just set it up as best you can, follow the technique, and observe everything without judgment or comment.

If you can get yourself established before the gong rings, you can use the ring down of the gong to seal you into your practice.

So that is the instruction on shamatha to begin with. If you want to practice shamatha regularly, it is important to relate with a properly trained meditation instructor. See Appendix C for suggestions.

Sitting at Home

In addition to group practice, I recommend practicing sitting meditation at home or work, whenever you can. It is good to set a specific amount of time at the outset of a session, anywhere from 5–25 minutes, and try to stick to that. Otherwise, your mind might be constantly trying the door handle to get off the cushion. Actually, your mind might be doing that either way. You can always stay longer, but don't make a contest out of it. Just try to stick it out for the amount of time you committed yourself to and also notice how your mind is with that.

Perhaps, needless to say it's probably good to start with shorter periods of 5–10 minutes and work your way up. Sitting in the morning or just at the same time each day can be helpful for keeping up your practice. I read somewhere that anything you do for six weeks running is easier to sustain. But don't be hard on yourself if you fall off your schedule, just don't give up! Group practice is very good for beginning and experienced practitioners.

Formal practice aside, you can and should synchronize your body and mind whenever it occurs to you. After all, that is what we are practicing for. Sometimes it helps to just zero in on any direct perception of your environment to settle yourself and then try to relax and open up to being fully present with whatever you are doing. So don't be picky about where and when to reel your consciousness in to just being where you are. And don't be affected when you are doing it. It's ordinary, and the more frequent the better, on a chair, on a cushion, while walking, running, working, anytime, all the time. Don't stop what you are doing, just be right there with it.

Formal practice aside, you can and should synchronize your body and mind whenever it occurs to you.

Finally, for formal sitting practice it is helpful to be looking at a fairly clean, well-lit, simple, uplifted space, maybe with a vase of fresh flowers in view, maybe a Buddha image and a votive candle or two if you can arrange it. We can talk about Buddhist shrine symbolism down the road, but basically you want to see things that remind you of the primordial purity of yourself and the world. Representations of nature or clarity—like fresh clear water—are good, perhaps a picture of an inspiring meditation teacher and/or a book that reminds you of your basic goodness. Avoid anything too complicated or personal. You want it to be uplifted because our minds tend to reflect whatever we are looking at sooner or later (which is also a good reason to put a plant and some art in your office!).

Appendix B:
The Context of Shamatha Meditation

Introduction to meditation instruction preceding The Third Noble Truth (of Wealth) *talk.*

The meditation technique that we have been practicing is called *shamatha*, which translates to "calm abiding" or resting the mind.

The idea of shamatha meditation is to create the simplest possible space or framework to objectively witness the comings and goings and general activity of our minds. Normally, we don't have a steady reference point against which to observe how mind works—how our thoughts progress, how our emotions come on and dissipate, all the different things that go on in there. Normally our thoughts are coaching us pretty much non-stop. Whatever's going on, we've got some kind of commentary filling up every available space, screening every experience for confirmations or threats to ego.

Normally our thoughts are coaching us pretty much non-stop.

So meditation is meant to create a space where we can watch the coach, or just be aware of the mental activity that goes on more objectively. It's hard to get "outside the box," entirely since we are kind of one with the box, but we can be a wallflower at the thought party, and thereby gain a much larger perspective. It's as simple as that.

As I have said before, shamatha is also known as formless meditation. It does have a technique when you are learning it: for example, how to sit, how to breathe, what to do with your eyes, etc. But this technique is actually very minimal compared to other forms of meditation, consequently, shamatha is considered to be quite advanced and challenging.

Also, in this tradition, we practice shamatha with our eyes open. That represents a further challenge, but makes it easier in some ways too. One benefit being that it is a step toward bringing mindfulness into everyday life.

The idea is to be very awake and present and relaxed at the same time.

Q. *How is shamatha different from vipassyana? Is that a kind of meditation as well? Did Trungpa also teach that lineage? I think I read about that. And how is that different?*
A. In the Shambhala tradition, shamatha, which is mindfulness oriented, is generally taught first; vipassyana, which is awareness oriented, you could say is a natural extension of mindfulness and shamatha.

Q. *Is there a direct relation with shamatha to the Hinayana (the path of simplicity) and vipassyana to the Mahayana (the highway of compassion)?*
A. I would say vipassyana is a step in that direction. I don't think it is a direct association, but there is a sense that one starts with simplicity and gradually expands to include more. It is critical to begin at the beginning though. Beginning at the beginning makes it possible to go farther in the end. As with any endeavor, if you skip the beginning you find yourself part way down the road spinning your wheels, and you don't know why. So it pays to get started properly.

On the spiritual path, we create a lot of space around what it is that we're trying to see or do. In the context of meditation practice, or in any part of life, if you create a lot of space around something, it's possible to understand it on a more subtle level.

If you create a lot of space around something,
it's possible to understand it on a more subtle level.

I used the example in the last class that it's like what a professional does. Just to keep our connection with economic life, that's what an accountant does, or a lawyer, or a carpenter—anybody who's an expert at anything. They create a big space around little details so they can see them in a more spacious context, and based on that wider perspective they can see clearly what to do. It's like looking through a magnifying glass or taking the pressure off a situation.

Beginning at the beginning has the quality of slowing down and taking your time. In meditation, like other things, you can and do get there through application and repetition. By just applying yourself to the technique over and over and over. Gradually you pick up a little bit more perspective each time. But repetition alone takes a long, long time. If you can slow down and surrender, i.e. apply Right Concentration in order to be with what you're doing, you can learn much faster. But that's easier said than done, hence the repetition.

Q. *One more question, just about the different varieties of meditation in this lineage. I don't really know much about meditation. I know very little. I've read a little bit. Are there certain times of the day, week, month that you personally would be doing vipassyana meditation, or are there other meditations that you also do at different times of the day, week, month? Or is shamatha a primary? Even though it's beginning or basic, can it be all-consuming? In other words, can it be a life practice? Because it seems like you have been practicing for a long*

time and you are still doing this basic practice, so it must be a strong practice.
Do you also do other practices as well? Or is this a core practice for you in
meditation specifically?

A. I think that formal meditation practice is like good hygiene,
something we are working with to better see our basic goodness/
inherent wealth. But there is also the opportunity to connect with
it in every moment of our lives. Every meditation practice has a
natural journey of its own. You might be doing mindfulness oriented shamatha practice, but over time there might be a quality
of vipassyana or awareness that begins to occur naturally with it.

To answer your question, yes there are different techniques and
other forms of meditation that are part of the Shambhala Buddhist
path and the Kagyü and Nyingma lineages of Tibetan Buddhism
that are its main tributaries. As a long-time student of all three of
those I can tell you that the basic object of synchronizing body
and mind as a means to unearthing basic goodness/Buddha nature,
or inherent wealth, as I am referring to it, is always the same.

There are meditation techniques that employ the use of mantras,
chants, visualizations and yoga to give our habitual mentalities a
lure or even a jolt toward a more uplifted way of looking at things.
But these practices almost always begin and end with a formless
meditation like shamatha. They are all techniques to help us see
and move our habitual mental projections a little more in line with
our inherently enlightened nature and the sacredness of our world
as it already is. The phenomenal world is prompting us in that
same way all the time. That is why it is said that the phenomenal
world is the ultimate teacher. But we are not always ready/willing
to receive its non-conceptual reminders.

Like all contemplative traditions, the Shambhala Buddhist path
incorporates teachings and introduces new meditation techniques
systematically over years of practice and study. One thing that
makes it special is that it is designed to be a full-fledged spiritual
path for householders. It is wonderful and also very challenging.

We don't talk about the, so called, advanced practices before their time because there is a lot of temptation to use spiritual techniques to reinforce ego i.e. without making a relationship to what Chögyam Trungpa called "groundlessness." Without that insight, spirituality becomes just another form of construction material to fortify ego. The genuine path is always here and now.

It is only when you actually make a connection with egoless-ness that genuine experience can come in. It's quite challenging to do that, from an egotistical point of view, because, "you can't witness your own funeral." So as genuine practitioners we have to embrace that uncertain, open space and see what happens. That is what shamatha practice is all about. It's a wholesome foundation and complete fruition practice at once.

> *It is only when you actually make a connection with egolessness that genuine experience can come in.*

In my experience what's important is to give in wholeheart-edly to the technique of the practice that you are doing. So I want everyone to try to follow the instruction I am going to give you as literally as you can. I recognize that there is a little faith, a little surrender required in that, but then surrender is part of it. We are taking a break from constantly coaching, manipulating, and strategizing our experience. We are going to just go with the flow, and trust our intelligence. It's not that wild a leap because, in this case, we are following the guidance of a 2,500-year-old living tradition.

In this particular instance, whatever you have learned before, or whatever little edits your mind thinks would make it a more com-fortable version for you in particular, please ignore them! Follow the technique as simply and closely as you can. Surrendering to just doing it is part of the challenge. Sticking to the technique is the best way to get good data, so to speak. So don't be self-critical, but do apply yourself. On the other hand, if you are having trouble with the practice you can discuss it with your meditation instructor who might recommend some accommodations or adjustments that would help without undermining it.

> *Sticking to the technique is the best way to get good data, so to speak.*

These meditation techniques and this path have been developed and updated since the time of the Buddha by people just like you and me who have gotten right into meditation practice; and this is what is being suggested to us at this point. It's as if our completely cheered-up relatives came from another planet where they understand mind like the Inuit understand snow, and, having already been where we are at some point, warts and all, they designed this for us. Make no mistake; even though shamatha seems basic, it is both the entry point and the fruition of the quick path to enlightenment.

Chögyam Trungpa, was a highly realized and respected Tantric Buddhist teacher and a passionate student of western mind, western culture. He chose very deliberately to teach shamatha to western students, not because this is how they do it in Tibetan monasteries, but because it hit the spot. The way we practice also reflects Zen-style instructions that he was aware of in part through his friendship with Suzuki Roshi, who wrote *Zen Mind, Beginner's Mind*. All of that and more went into why he felt western students should begin with shamatha. He was criticized initially because some traditional Tibetan Buddhist teachers thought he trusted western students and himself way too much. But now his teachings are the gold standard for Tibetan Buddhist teachers seeking ways to convey the heart of the Buddha dharma to western students. Finally, I can say from my own experience, shamatha is great.

So to continue with the instruction, shamatha meditation begins with taking your seat on your cushion or on your chair, whatever you are sitting on.

Q. *Layth, where did you get your cushion? Because that looks like a good one.*
A. I got my cushion from Samadhi Cushions in Vermont, and I am very eager to help people get cushions. The boxy rectangular cushion I am sitting on is called a "gomden" and it was designed for westerners by Chögyam Trungpa. The mat underneath it is called a "zabutan". I think getting your own meditation cushions is a key milestone of a good personal practice; and also, cushions are a big step toward building a meditation group. (See link to Samadhi Cushions in Appendix C.)

Years ago, I led an outreach program in Fredericton, New Brunswick. On a whim I decided to sell the 10 or 12 sets of used meditation cushions I brought with me to the participants. They all sold in less than a minute! I got in big trouble back in Halifax for doing that because good meditation cushions don't grow on trees you know. But now they have a thriving meditation center there. I like to think those cushions gave them a boost.

Appendix C: Suggested Websites

All contemplative traditions help to uplift human society through pure perception and transcending ego fixation. Contemplative practice helps us trust our own awareness and intelligence over habitual or dogmatic prejudice.

If you would like to learn more about the traditions I have followed, I recommend reading books by any of the teachers listed in the acknowledgements.

Here are some websites you may wish to visit.

www.shambhala.org

www.victoria.shambhala.org

www.nalandabodhi.org

To order meditation cushions and other practice materials:

www.samadhicushions.com

For more information and to contact the author please visit:

www.enlightenedeconomy.com

or

www.ratemiser.ca

Afterword about Chögyam Trungpa Rinpoche and Shambhala

Chögyam Trungpa Rinpoche was a classically trained Tibetan Buddhist meditation master. Recognized as the 11th reincarnation of a great teacher at a young age, he was trained by some of the greatest Tibetan Buddhist teachers of our time: Jamgön Kongtrül of Shechen, Khenpo Gangshar Rinpoche, H.H. Dilgo Khyentse, H.H. Rangjung Rigpe Dorje the 16th Karmapa, and, Surmang Rolpa Dorje, to name a few. By the time he was in his teens he had become a respected teacher in his own right and the head of Surmang Monastery in eastern Tibet.

The Chinese invasion forced him to flee Tibet in 1959. When he reached India in 1960, H.H. the Dalai Lama appointed him spiritual advisor to the Young Lamas Home School in Dalhousie, India. There he began to master the English language and in 1963 received a scholarship to Oxford where he studied comparative religion.

Trungpa Rinpoche was fascinated with the etymology of words, the elocution of speech, and all nuances of western culture in the 1960s, 70s, and 80s. When his profound grasp of Buddhism connected with his study of the western mindset, he became an extraordinary source of spiritual insight in the West.

Confidence in his own understanding combined with desire to transplant the genuine heart of Buddhism, led him to bring forth timely wisdom and develop new ways of presenting the spiritual journey customized to the needs of westerners. He called this new cultural and educational approach Shambhala Training, which is meant to present a non-sectarian contemplative training for people of any tradition. Shambhala Training is now complemented by a series of connecting classes and called the Way of Shambhala, which is the core curriculum of the Shambhala Buddhist lineage under the leadership of Sakyong Mipham Rinpoche. Sakyong Mipham is the son of Trungpa Rinpoche and was thoroughly trained by him, H.H. Dilgo Khyentse Rinpoche, and other great masters to be the leader of Shambhala.

The Shambhala approach is distinguished by regarding all aspects of society as sacred, legitimate, and part of the spiritual path.

The Shambhala approach is distinguished
by regarding all aspects of society as sacred,
legitimate, and part of the spiritual path.

Chögyam Trungpa developed contemplative forms and non-aggressive approaches to many institutions-including the military! He also remained vigilant of the habitual mind's temptation to make spiritual practice into just another credential for propping up ego. He addressed this latter point in many ways entitling one of his early books, *Cutting Through Spiritual Materialism*, and emphasizing its significance throughout his teachings.

Trungpa Rinpoche developed the Shambhala Training curriculum to be a personal path of contemplative training for citizens of an enlightened society.

The cultural/sociological approach of Shambhala is based upon some of the most profound teachings of Buddhism and other contemplative traditions. It is a living tradition so it is continuously updating and adapting and training new teachers and leaders. It incorporates ancient and modern disciplines such as flower arranging, calligraphy, tea ceremony, contemplative archery, photography, art, and martial arts. Chögyam Trungpa also recognized the potential of elocution, etiquette, and seasonal celebration as opportunities to practice mindfulness/awareness and uplift human society.

The implications of Trungpa Rinpoche's cultural approach are profound. If one can bridge mindfulness/awareness practice into daily activity, the spiritual journey continues 24/7. Shambhala lineage practitioners experience this continual practice more in the form of a switch of allegiance to wakefulness than being on constant guard against neurosis. If basic goodness/inherent wealth is home, all one needs to do is relax to arrive there. In fact, we are all returning home to basic goodness (AKA the enlightened state) briefly all the time without recognizing it.

---

*If basic goodness/inherent wealth is home,
all one needs to do is relax to arrive there.*

With limitless curiosity and appreciation, Trungpa Rinpoche borrowed liberally from the Zen tradition, Japanese contemplative arts, and from other schools of Buddhism in crafting the spacious and elegant Shambhala approach for westerners. He created a powerful yet accessible spiritual path to guide us toward the essence of cheerfulness, free of excessive exoticism, which he felt was a big distraction from the heart of the teachings.

Chögyam Trungpa Rinpoche died on April 4th, 1987 but his humor and insight still permeate everyone who practices and studies his teachings. With the help of well-trained senior students and Acharyas (senior teachers), Sakyong Mipham is extending the Shambhala tradition to all who wish to explore it.

Whether one is attracted to the Shambhala approach or not, the practice of creating enlightened society by helping human beings discover their basic goodness is available at any contemplative center near you. Respect for the primordial purity of all beings and a generous sense of humor are all that is required.

The essential message of Chögyam Trungpa Rinpoche was threefold:

1. All sentient beings are basically good—meaning we are all inherently pure, brilliant, communicative, and thus workable.

2. Sanity is based on, genuine prosperity arises from, and enlightened society is created by, connecting with this ground of basic goodness/inherent wealth.

3. The way to connect with basic goodness is by synchronizing body and mind, and the practice of sitting meditation is the best foundation for doing that.

Afterword about Economics

In an audience with the late Amteng Yogi, one of the most respected yogis of the Kagyü Lineage of Tibetan Buddhism, I asked for his advice on how to combine business with Dharma (commerce and wisdom). After a bit of discussion in Tibetan, his translator turned back to me with a concerned look and said, "Rinpoche says it is not possible to combine business with Dharma." After some unsatisfying discourse, I went away a little shocked. My teacher, Chögyam Trungpa Rinpoche, had always told us we could and should bring our mindfulness and awareness practice into every aspect of our lives. So at first I thought that maybe Amteng Yogi just didn't understand.

Reflecting over time however, I came to see Amteng's point. Business is concerned with the pragmatics of prosperity in this life, and the Buddhadharma offers a view that informs this life, but transcends the limits of material advantage. So I realized that you cannot combine business with dharma, but you can conduct business in a dharmic (profound) way. In other words, we can allow our mindfulness and awareness, to infiltrate our daily activities and thereby imbue them with wisdom, humor, and inspiration of a higher order. The economic system reflects and distributes this. In this way I believe a widespread understanding of inherent wealth would have profound positive ripple effects throughout society.

At first blush, some economists will have just as much trouble as Amteng Yogi did in reconciling the subjective approach of contemplative arts with a field so eager for objective benchmarks. But understanding the economic decision-making process demands more than a mechanistic frame of reference. In other words, you can't ignore the subtler inspiration of the individual or the population if you are going to predict outcomes or set down good policy.

So I realized that you cannot combine business with dharma, but you can conduct business in a dharmic (profound) way.

It's hard for policy makers and economists to incorporate this. But as an example, many companies have found good results from harnessing the altruism of customers and employees for the welfare of larger groups, creating a sense of partnership. Another example of such heroism is the high-income earners supporting progressive tax rates. Which suggests a positive relationship between income and empathy, or is it the other way round? Either way, such sentiments suggest a transcendent understanding of wealth. Whatever your stance on tax policy may be, the Buddhist view is that actions taken with altruistic aspirations have a multiplier effect.

The problem has always been that the inspiration of the population is hard to characterize or quantify, much less transform with or without aggression. But that doesn't mean it is not a critical factor in determining why one individual/organization/community/economy will rebound and another will struggle under similar circumstances/policy. I read a case study in university about teachers in Soviet Russia who continued to teach school even when they received only Samovars as pay. Neighbors come out of the woodwork to help each other whenever a natural disaster shuts our televisions down. Un-inspired approaches to commerce and entertainment put a drag on creativity and the whole world economy with it. Inspired activity uplifts the whole world with it too.

The self-awareness of the population and the leadership are as important as gas and oil to an economic engine. It's tempting to focus on manipulating the logic of economic and justice policy or organizational incentive plans, but in reality, the leadership of self-empowered individuals is the key and most powerful source of inspiration available to man. We've always assumed it was slavery but now some think it more likely that inspiration built the Pyramids. Either way, the correct number of leaders in an organization of 108 is 108. You can't get healthy morale by manipulating policy alone. People must have heart for things. I actually think the word nobility is a better term for what we are looking for than leadership because the latter implies a value system based on how many reports.

*The self-awareness of the population
and the leadership are as important as
gas and oil to an economic engine.*

If people are inspired by their personal role in creating enlightened society, many economic systems will work. And the reverse is also true. We should not assume we are helpless to change things or inspire others on the personal level just because of our salary level or place in the organizational chart. In my experience contemplative training transforms any situation from the center or the fringe. That is because greater awareness provides the consideration and perception of new options and inspiration to explore them. Even more significant, awareness reveals the sacredness of things as they are.

What you can see clearly in volunteer organizations is that the leadership/nobility of individual group members determines the best fit leadership style of formal leaders and the viability of strategic options as much, if not more than environmental factors.

"Ask not what your country can do for you..." Recognizing the power of far-sighted inspiration reveals the benefits of larger minded projects locally as well as globally—including some that may seem "impractical" but work for the heart. Mass transit and environmental projects come to mind, but what about inspiration based initiatives? E.g. building a giant statue as a state gift for a fledgling democracy, like France did for the United States all those years ago? Or even for a trading partner for that matter. Wouldn't have to cost that much, wouldn't have a direct economic payoff, but it could raise a lot of spirits and have a great peace dividend. Hence the long-term economic payoff would actually be spectacular, just not easily measured within one economy or political term. This is what makes a gift genuine, almost by definition. It is also the nature of genuine nobility and art. A genuine gift is a product of inspiration not a loan against some future payoff. The same principle can be applied to organizing excellent company celebrations and dinner parties.

From an economic point of view enlarging a network and improving communication between the nodes on the network, geometrically expands its potential value. In other words, wider and better communication is a source of economic efficiency and prosperity. If our response to fear and pain is to seek greater awareness it serves to update and expand the network. Defensive reactions reduce communication and diversity and so undercut prosperity.

The recognition that all human beings are basically good by nature, forms the basis to recognize the beating hearts of other organizations and societies as well and so unleash better cross-cultural communication as a powerful economic driver. Otherwise, we are effectively waiting for a day when fear or greed recklessly unifies or divides us. In other words, we should recognize the inspirational and economic benefits of reducing political/organizational boundaries and not isolate ourselves so much.

On the other hand, anything that undermines communication and trust, like building gigantic fences and weaponizing drones, reflects ignorance of the common heroic nature of all human beings and proactively obscures it, which is disastrous for humanity. This will stunt healthy economic activity, feed ignorance of the environment, and rationalize more aggression. One side of the divide becomes more precious, ignorant, and defensive, while the other becomes more wretched and justifiably self-righteous. There are better ways to fight fires than pouring gasoline on them from 1,000 feet.

We should recognize the inspirational and economic benefits of reducing political/organizational boundaries and not isolate ourselves so much.

But diffusing aggression and building bridges requires more exposure not less. Once we refuse to be open with each other, progress comes to a halt. If we invested equally in aid, education, and exchange programs as we do in defense the payoffs would be multi-generational too. Looking past issues to commonalities is a more effective place to start a conversation because it is a more effective approach.

In the Shambhala community we use the term "creating enlightened society" like a verb describing any uplifted unifying activity. Creating enlightened economy is an easy entry point to creating enlightened society just as inherent wealth is an aspect of what we call basic goodness—the unconditionally pure nature of human beings.

In the Shambhala community we use the term "creating enlightened society" like a verb describing any uplifted unifying activity.

In the political economy of ego, collective momentum only seems to reach critical mass in response to major external threats exemplified by the "War on Terror" or collective manias like the technology boom. The contemplative approach is to establish means to continuously re-discover our inherent creativity as individuals free of divisive identities and expand out from there through the fearless appreciation of the same in others.

One way to address the collective patterns of greed and fear is to experiment with the energetic, health, and productivity benefits of contemplative practices, like meditation, on organizational and municipal scales. Every home or office building begs for a quiet, elegant space with some flowers and meditation cushions as much as a gym. If that seems fantastical, look at the widespread practice of Tai Chi in Chinese society. Many western educational and other institutions are experimenting pro-actively with contemplative programming now.

Every home or office building begs for a
quiet, elegant space with some flowers and
meditation cushions as much as a gym.

The contemplative contribution to economic development could be characterized as recognizing the extraordinary value of mental health. This can be done through support for contemplative arts, recreation, or any local cultural activity that fosters self-awareness, communication, and trust, which are also the seeds of sustainable economic activity. Jane Jacobs emphasizes the contribution of the arts, local traditions, and crafts to engendering the culture of entrepreneurship and urban renewal in her book Cities and the Wealth of Nations. Facilitating entrepreneurship in the arts e.g. theatre companies, concerts, art showings and other performances, or contemplative arts events, environmental and recreational volunteerism in any sphere, is an excellent way to challenge and train people of all ages, locally and globally. The virtue of contemplative training is that it trains us to work with the merits of each situation vs. inflexible rule structures.

All of this can be brought down to the household level for example in the form of a welcoming dinner party, which could be a microcosm of enlightened society with the potential to transform human existence. Just expand the perimeter of the guest list a little outside the comfort zone and practice deep listening.

Societal economic growth can be viewed through the same lens that we used to examine fear and pain vs. panic and suffering. When we regard fear and pain as ordinary they are interesting and informative, when we over-react and pretend that it should be possible to avoid every uncomfortable experience, we get stuck with panic and suffering. The 9/11 attacks were a message that needed to be responded to on many levels: security, justice, diplomacy, human relations, mental health, and international aid. But how we distribute our focus between and apply ourselves to these different responses reflects our wealthy or defensive outlook, which in turn creates its own transformative opportunities or fallout.

Societal economic growth can be viewed through the same lens that we used to examine fear and pain vs. panic and suffering.

Since we are enriched through communication and trust, sister cities projects and exchange programs are an example of initiatives with promise to expand awareness through cross-cultural friendship. The idea of fostering innovation and technology transfer by facilitating friendships between professionals in similar trades across economic boundaries based on mutual respect is interesting. The "developed" country can share technology; the "less developed country" can share resourcefulness and both can gain innovation.

The huge contribution that inspired ethics make to productivity should not be overlooked. High minded but practical political frameworks such as the US Constitution and globally aware statements of corporate social responsibility should be understood to be not only guardians of justice, but guidelines for sustainable inspiration and productivity too.

The huge contribution that inspired ethics make to productivity should not be overlooked.

The problem with the corporate business model is not that it is small minded, as it is often accused. In fact, the corporate business model has been instrumental in distributing material wealth wider and faster than at any time in world history. The problem is that there remains ignorance of collateral side effects such as environmental destruction because business and even national motivation is still group focused and thus egocentrically shortsighted. Innovation seeking corporations can benefit greatly from establishing global social welfare objectives and contemplative training to connect their activity with vaster vision. Even if it may seem like wishful thinking at first, we shouldn't be cynical, the human mind is highly innovative over time.

Ultimately, it is the sustained inspiration of individuals that creates economic momentum. The inspiration of a good song or a rousing speech can get us on our feet but we need to understand ourselves on a deeper level in order to access it again and again. An enlightened society is one that celebrates all the different ways that individuals can connect to basic goodness and express their genuine inspiration through whatever they are doing, one moment at a time.

Ultimately, it is the sustained inspiration of individuals that creates economic momentum.

The Relationship of Income and Well-Being

The Income vs. Well-being chart depicts the general relationship of income and well-being in two cases: with and without the benefit of meditation or other forms of contemplative mind training.

Income vs. Well-being

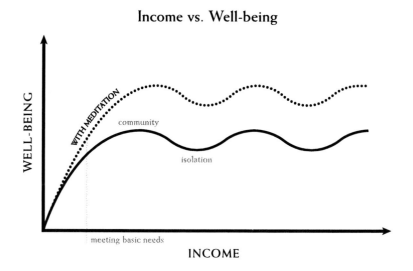

As you can see, well-being rises very directly with increased income to the level of meeting basic needs, meaning sufficient funds to sustain adequate food, shelter, health, and safety in a given society. Contemplative training helps individuals find well-being a little sooner under adverse circumstances, through wider awareness and because one learns to seek it more directly e.g. deferring consumption strategically, sharing information and resources more readily, clearer distinctions between wants and needs.

Once basic needs are met, the benefits of additional income start to diverge but still vary cyclically with or without meditation. The utility of income peaks at what I call the "potluck" or "community" stage, meaning the point where there are sufficient resources and leisure to participate fully in a given social strata. But as income continues to rise it results in increasing isolation due to divergent circumstances and aspirations with the social group until a new community situation or relationship is arrived at, and on it goes. So by my chart, lottery winners would experience an immediate loss of well-being due to the isolation effect of sudden wealth.

Lottery winners would experience an immediate loss of well-being due to the isolation effect of sudden wealth.

As income rises the aspirations and opportunities to pursue self-actualization expand, but the level of personal well-being remains cyclical and does not necessarily rise overall unless there is an expansion of insight into the nature of mind. Mind is just doing its thing with the new set of toys and aspirations that increased income affords.

The implication for researchers and policy makers is to explore the limitations of focusing on income outcomes alone and to recognize the self-defeating effects of delivery systems that drag down the needy with onerous hurdles to sustain themselves. The ROI of shifting focus to projects that create inspiration, as well as employment may be much higher over time and create a more diverse skill base.

The broken line on the income vs. well-being chart represents the addition of psychological self-awareness into the equation. Such insight is gained most directly through sitting meditation. This additional perspective on the nature of mind has the potential to increase the utility of income because a more experience focused value system will result in using additional income to facilitate deeper insight into one's perception/experience. E.g. supporting the leisure time for meditation practice and retreats, complemented by the occasional cooking class. Deferring consumption is also easier with a greater sense of inherent wealth/wholeness. As egocentric fixations come down, there is a heightened sense of common experience with others. You could call this recognition of interdependence, or sacredness, which contributes to well-being directly. This would also tend to smooth the highs and lows associated with changes in income levels, although the chart does not reflect this.

Deferring consumption is also easier with a greater sense of inherent wealth/wholeness.

Nevertheless, even in the "with meditation" scenario, the benefit of additional income plateaus fairly early on the income spectrum for meditators as well. In other words, the income itself ceases to make incremental contributions beyond a certain level. The only way to achieve higher levels of well-being from the Buddhist perspective is through the dawn of wisdom and compassion, which you could say heightens the sense of community to its limit AKA enlightenment, but has no predictable relationship to income. Also, the chart does not reflect that variations in income can be excellent training grounds for those who seek a more transcendent understanding of prosperity.

This chart is only a sketch to illustrate the potential benefit of focusing on the experiential or "spiritual" approach to wealth. Everyone's experience varies. Increased personal discipline and virtue will tend to help anyone enjoy life more in the short-run. But it is only insight into the nature of mind that brings lasting relief from the suffering that accompanies an egocentric outlook.

It is only insight into the nature of mind that brings lasting relief from the suffering that accompanies an egocentric outlook.

Acknowledgements

I offer this book to all the compassionate wisdom beings across time, culture, and spirit. Please grant your blessings so that human beings may create enlightened society together. May the dark ignorance of sentient beings be dispelled. May all beings enjoy profound, brilliant, glory.

The principal source of any insight here was my original teacher, The Venerable Chögyam Trungpa Rinpoche (Rinpoche is an honorific which means precious teacher) and the Kagyü and Nyingma lineage masters of Tibetan Buddhism that he introduced us to including: His Holiness Dilgo Khyentse Rinpoche, H.H. Rangjung Rikpe Dorje Rinpoche the 16th Karmapa, His Eminence Jamgön Kongtrül Rinpoche, Khenchen Thrangu Rinpoche, Kyabje Tenga Rinpoche, Kalu Rinpoche, and many others.

Everything I have learned flowed through the window of my own contemplative practice and study, which I opened with the guidance of the senior students of Trungpa Rinpoche. In particular, I was lucky to study with the Vajra Regent Ösel Tendzin, who wrote *Buddha in the Palm of Your Hand*. He was an extraordinary teacher, with a warm heart, and integral to establishing the worldwide Shambhala Mandala.

Sakyong Mipham Rinpoche, the eldest son of Trungpa Rinpoche and now leader of the Shambhala Buddhist Lineage, has been my teacher since his father's death in 1987. He has written many books including The Shambhala Principle. He is the best example of enlightened leadership I have ever seen.

The Dzogchen Ponlop Rinpoche has also been my teacher and a great source of inspiration to me for many years. Ponlop

Rinpoche's books: *Wild Awakening* and *Mind Beyond Death* were great references for many of my comments here. Whenever I think of him my heart is filled with joy.

Khenpo Tsultrim Gyamtso Rinpoche, Chagdud Tulku Rinpoche, Khenpo Karthar Rinpoche, Shunryu Suzuki Roshi, Kanjuro Shibata Sensei, Dzongsar Khyentse Rinpoche, Tulku Urgyen Rinpoche, and many other brilliant teachers from diverse spiritual lineages have all contributed profoundly to the studies of myself, and fellow western students over the years.

I wish to acknowledge H.H. Tenzin Gyatso the 14th Dalai Lama and H.H. Ogyen Trinley Dorje the 17th Karmapa who are the best living examples of unconditional compassion in the world today.

The Dorje Loppön Lodro Dorje has been spiritual friend and mentor to me within the Shambhala mandala since the 1980s. Ane Pema Chödrön and my fellow meditation practitioners of the Seattle, Karmè Chöling, Halifax, Victoria, and international Shambhala communities have been my constant companions and a vast bank of experience for the ideas in this book and much more.

My late dear mother, Dr. Hind Kadry Matthews and my wonderful father, Dr. Ahmed Thomas James Matthews trained me in equanimity and showed me the meaning of unconditional love and selfless generosity by example.

I wish to thank my cousin, Tom Strickland, through who's friendship I discovered the Buddhist path and who himself is a great example of generosity beyond the limits ego.

My Canadian mortgage and investment clients have shared their varied experiences of economic life so generously over the years I could not help but discover a few common themes to share.

I would like to thank my editor, Julia Fabian, whose upbeat ideas, genuine curiosity, and lightning fast turnaround helped me to clarify my voice despite the esoteric nature of the subject matter.

Dr. Jim Sacamano encouraged me by example and shared his humor and insights on the journey to publishing his own book

Getting Back to Wholeness: The Treasure of Inner Health and the Power of a Meaningful Life.

I send a big thanks to my readers Patricia O'Byrne and Cheryl Sacamano who held their tongues on the early drafts and gave me great edits and nothing but encouragement.

A great big thank you to Silas Rosenblatt, my contemplative comrade, acupuncturist, and social entrepreneur who helped me with the cover and website design. www.DesignVictoria.ca

Tashi Mannox the professional artist, and one time Kagyü Buddhist monk, not only advised us on appropriate symbolism and calligraphy, but also created the wish-fulfilling Jewel with JAM syllable stamp on the cover especially for me. The wish fulfilling jewel is compassion and the JAM is the seed syllable for wealth, so combined it means wealth in the context of compassion. Tashi cheered us on readily even though we approached him as complete strangers. www.TashiMannox.com

The magical windhorse emblem on the back cover is a version of a brilliant stained glass work by Alice L. Johnson. The windhorse symbolizes the energy that springs forth from the synchronization of body and mind. You can see the original image on her website www.alice-johnson.com. Alice graciously gave her permission to use it conditional upon the consent of the owner, Ricky Bernstein, who is an artist himself and also sponsors an NGO supporting literacy for girls in the Kathmandu valley. www.handsinoutreach.org

Thank you to Fiona Raven Book Design who helped me with book layout and graphic design, and advised me patiently through the self-publishing maze. www.fionaraven.com

My good friends Aaron Whitman and Troy Woodland at Able Sense Media Inc. applied their excellent media skills and extraordinary patience to help me produce the Income vs. Well-Being chart in readable format. www.ablesense.com

Mandy Leith's combined enthusiasm for spirituality and economics made her the obvious choice for helping me to promote this book. www.MediaRising.ca

I would also like to thank: Tenzin Chokey, the Tibetan refuge village of Tashi Jong, Acharya Larry Mermelstein, Robert Reichner, Mark Hazell, Becky Hazell, Charles Blackhall, Gerrit Gosker, Maryanne Treverow, John Cowan, Henri van Amerongen, Katia Schokalska, Hisako Yoshida, Haytham Matthews, Jeff Matthews, Janet Jonak, Ron Hilburn, Finley (Ted) Clarke, Robert Kennedy, Jesse Domingue, John O'Dea, Dave Griswald, Ginny Guthrie, Kerry Crofton, Sonia Felix, Cameron Wenaus, David Griffiths, Ken Tobias, Charlie Comstock, Ngawang Choedon, Acharya Susan Chapman, Iryna Spica, members of the Victoria Shambhala Council, David Brown, Acharya Arawana Hayashi, and Carolyn Mendelker and many more who all helped and encouraged me in small and large ways.

Finally, I wish to thank my three wonderful children, Thomas, Tara, and Dylan for their mirthful encouragement and for accommodating those many days and nights I was away from home practicing, studying, teaching, or cloistered in my office writing.

The biggest thank you of all to my lovely wife Trudy, who puts up with me and surrounds me with love and encouragement whilst keeping my feet firmly on the ground.

May all my teachers, family, and supporters, named and unnamed, be pleased with this book. May it be a useful reference for anyone wishing to discover prosperity and create enlightened society.

About the Author

Layth Matthews has been studying Buddhism and economics since 1979. He has been an authorized teacher and meditation instructor in the Shambhala Buddhist tradition since 1989. He is an active Shambhala Training director and leads meditation retreats across North America. He is also a former Centre Director of the Victoria Shambhala Centre in Victoria, British Columbia where he lives with his wife and three children.

Layth is Senior Mortgage Advisor & CEO of RateMiser Mortgage Advisors, a Canadian mortgage brokerage. He has also been a business development manager, financial journalist, and an investment advisor. He has taught finance at Dalhousie Business School and mortgage brokerage at Nova Scotia Community College.

Layth studied economics at the University of Washington and Harvard and has an MBA from Dalhousie University. He is often recognized for economic insight and leadership within the Shambhala community. He is an active member of the Shambhala Business Model Optimization Team and the Enlightened Economy Group.

He can be reached via email at: layth@enlightenedeconomy.com

It is hoped that *The Four Noble Truths of Wealth: a Buddhist view of economic life* will open the door to a wealthy outlook for people of every faith and persuasion.

Whatever the virtues of the many fields of knowledge,
All are steps on the path of omniscience.
May these arise in the clear mirror of intellect,
O Manjushri, please accomplish this.

H.H. Dilgo Khyentse Rinpoche

CPSIA information can be obtained
at www.ICGtesting.com
Printed in the USA
FSOW01n0500060116
15186FS